by Joel Henning

IMPROVING LAWYER PRODUCTIVITY

How to Train, Manage and Supervise your Lawyers

LawLetters, Inc.
332 South Michigan Avenue
Chicago, Illinois 60604

Library of Congress Card Catalogue Number: 85-080636
ISBN 0-914239-03-1

LawLetters, Inc., 332 South Michigan Avenue,
Chicago, Illinois 60604

First edition
Printed in the United States of America

Most of the chapters in this book appeared originally in
similar form in the *Lawyer Hiring & Training Report*, a
monthly newsletter published by LawLetters, Inc. of
Chicago.

Design by Joan Booz Design, Chicago

To Justine, Sarah-Anne and Dara.

Introduction

Six years ago when we created Joel Henning & Associates and LawLetters, Inc., we thought we were involved in traditional continuing legal education for presentation in the firms that had expanded so rapidly during the 1970s. It took a long time for us to realize that CLE was only part of the action.

Conceptually, we were pioneers in the field of lawyer development. That includes recruitment, hiring, orientation, mentoring, CLE, work assignments, supervision, feedback, on-the-job training, practice management skills, and the like.

CLE is important, but not in itself very interesting. Professional development is a vast, complex, and challenging field. There is much we still don't know. So don't expect this book to be definitive or comprehensive. It merely reflects what has come to my attention and caught my fancy in the past few years.

From time to time, I take a crack at writing the great American novel. It's far from finished. I also divert myself by writing occasional articles on the performing arts and physical fitness. As far as I know, I'm the only practicing lawyer who has published a book on running (*Holistic Running*, New American Library, 1978). IMPROVING LAWYER PRODUCTIVITY isn't anything like the great American novel or *Holistic Running*. This book is a collection of my accumulated writings over the past several years on the subjects of practice management and lawyer training.

The trouble with a book of collected writings is that it tends to be uneven and occasionally repetitive. This one suffers from both; the benefit of such a collection is that it brings together the writer's accumulated thinking on a sharply focused subject. Taken as a whole, a good collection can help the reader understand what's going on in a given field. Some of the points I repeat bear repeating.

Here's another interesting aspect of collected writings: they illustrate the evolution of the author's writing style. Sooner or later you are likely to come across my chapter dealing with clinical skills teaching techniques. I wrote this piece 10 years ago. Although I wrote most of the book in the past three years, that older piece is everything I rail against in the chapter on legal writing. It often is abstract, turgid, convoluted, legalistic, and soporific. On rediscovering it, my first inclination was to rewrite it completely. But then I decided to let it run more or less as is. It tells you what you need to know before teaching in a clinical teaching workshop. You just have to exert more effort to reach the good stuff. It should make you very alert to the difference between good and bad writing. If I can improve, so can you and your colleagues.

My professional life is mainly consumed with consulting and writing about practice management and lawyer training. Consultants and writers talk to lots of people. Most of what I know comes from talking to lawyers and other concerned professionals. Most of the people I talk to professionally worry a lot about lawyer training, and work hard to improve it. This book could not have been strung together without the insights and experiences that all of these worriers have shared with me. If I started to list them, you would think this is a telephone directory. I thank them all.

Contents

Contents

Supervising and Mentoring Younger Lawyers

Teaching Practical Skills

Why In-House Training is Necessary

Bye Bye Burger & Bok: What's Really Wrong With Lawyer Training?

> And he says: Now, these kittens, they do not get trained
> As we did in the days when Victoria reigned.
> They never get drilled in a regular troupe,
> And they think they are smart, just to jump through a hoop.
> *From "Gus the Theatre Cat," by T. S. Eliot*

The old Toms in every profession think that the kittens are not as competent as they used to be. Law is no exception. Led first by the Chief Justice of the United States and more recently by the President of Harvard University, the old Toms have railed against the training of American lawyers with the same passion, if not the same poetry that Gus the Theatre Cat directed at modern training of theater kittens. But the old Toms of the American legal profession point the finger at problems that don't exist, or the wrong problems, while the most important failures in how we train lawyers have thus far gone mostly undetected and uncorrected.

Burger and Bok: Misguided Critics of Lawyer Training

More than 20 years ago, Chief Justice Burger began alleging

This chapter began life as a paper prepared for the 23rd Australian Legal Convention at which I spoke in the summer of 1985. I hate footnotes. But in this case I have retained them because you may want to have a look at the references.

that the trial bar is — to a very alarming extent — unable to try cases.[1] More recently Harvard President Derek Bok, a former Harvard Law School Dean and Professor, has suggested that we have too many lawyers. Bok's view on training these hordes is in some respects at odds with the Chief Justice's. President Bok argues that law schools overemphasize "preparing students for legal combat" while ignoring "the gentler arts of reconciliation and accommodation."[2] Here are two of the most prominent members of the American bar, one complaining that we lawyers don't know how to try cases, the other that we know nothing but how to try cases.

I will not attempt to defend either the Chief Justice or the president of my alma mater: they are powerfully equipped to defend themselves. And, frankly, I am proletarian enough to be skeptical of criticism aimed at lawyers in the trenches delivered from the Olympian heights of the U.S. Supreme Court and the presidency of Harvard. Chief justices and university presidents using their offices to condemn lawyer training puts me in mind of the trial of Alice in Wonderland:

"What do you know about this business?" the King said to Alice.

"Nothing," said Alice.

"Nothing whatever?" persisted the King.

"Nothing whatever," said Alice.

"That's very important," the King said, turning to the jury.

As far as I can tell, the American trial bar is nowhere near as incompetent as Chief Justice Burger alleges. Many leading litigators agree with me.[3] At a minimum, our trial bar is as competent as the American trial bench.

President Bok has savaged — each in its turn — every profession with a graduate school at Harvard. His real mission, I think, is to convince all professionals — doctors, business executives, engineers, architects, and lawyers alike — to pay less attention to private clients and more to managing society. A. Bartlett Giamatti, the outgoing president of Yale University, said recently that "At Harvard all problems are viewed as political and susceptible to a public policy solution."[4] While Bok's may be a noble aim, it is well beyond the scope of this book — indeed beyond my imagination. Many think it is also beyond President Bok's purview.

What Lawyers Do and How They Learn to Do It

I think the problem of effective lawyer training is very real and very urgent but that it has not been accurately formulated by either the Chief Justice or President Bok. Stated simply, formal legal education focuses on only a few lawyering skills — however relevant — while ignoring many that lawyers themselves think most important to the practice of law. Furthermore, those skills that lawyers believe to be most important cannot be effectively taught in law school: they are acquired mostly through on-the-job training. So, to a large extent, we lawyers cannot escape from our individual and collective responsibility for lawyer training.

Few of the great leaders or thinkers in the legal profession have thought much about what lawyers actually do. But a 1981 study by the American Bar Foundation focused precisely on this question.[5] Not surprisingly, it found that "many of the skills considered most important to legal practice are not traditionally part of law school curricula."[6]

In the Bar Foundation study, almost 70 percent of the practicing lawyers surveyed considered "fact gathering" as the single most important lawyering skill. What most struck its authors was the fact that the four skills seen as extremely important by the largest proportion of legal practitioners — "fact gathering," "capacity to marshall facts and order them so that concepts can be applied," "instilling others' confidence in you," and "effective oral expression" — are not peculiar to the legal profession. One might as well be listing the most important skills needed by corporate executives, television news analysts, or psychiatrists. As these skills are not unique to the legal profession, we can hardly expect law schools to have anything special to offer in teaching them.

It's only when we get to the five skills ranked below the top four that we find more obvious links to the practice of law. They are "ability to understand and interpret opinions, regulations, and statutes," "knowledge of the substantive law," "legal research," "negotiating," and "drafting legal documents." According to the lawyers surveyed, law schools are capable of teaching only a few of the nine "extremely important" skills: fact gathering, effective oral expression, and drafting legal documents. Moreover, these lawyers perceive that law schools fail to teach even these skills well.[7]

The authors conclude that law schools emphasize a cluster of purely analytic skills to the virtual exclusion of the interpersonal skills that are at least equally central to the practice of law. And they say that law schools are not seen by lawyers to do a terribly good job even with those analytic skills. Furthermore, since the analytic skills are not equally important throughout the profession, law schools provide better preparation for some specialties than for others. I would venture that the smaller the law firm a new lawyer joins, the greater will be the need for interpersonal or "human" skills. If law schools fail to adequately teach these skills, graduates entering small firms or solo practice are at a very great disadvantage because they have the fewest opportunities for on-the-job training.

It's a mistake, however, to think that interpersonal skills are needed only by lawyers in smaller firms — those that represent persons rather than institutions. Because interpersonal skills are needed to train lawyers as well as to practice law, they are essential to those senior lawyers in larger firms responsible for training and supervising young lawyers.

The American Bar Foundation study should lay to rest the notion that legal education most notably neglects advocacy skills, as the Chief Justice has insisted, or other technical skills, as President Bok believes. Instead, United States legal education seems unable to deliver adequate training in interpersonal skills and — it should be added — professional responsibility. The uproar over the Chief Justice's attacks on the trial bar led him to appoint a committee to make formal recommendations on the problem of competence in trial skills. Ironically, the committee reported that the most frequent cause of inadequate trial performance is not a lack of technical skill but "failure by lawyers to prepare cases to the best of their ability."[8]

In fact, most clear cases of lawyer failure involve inattention, laziness, the press of other work, economic factors, or mistakes. These may relate to professional irresponsibility, but none reaches the level of lawyer competence. Yet in some states, the entire bar must submit to cosmetic gestures such as mandatory continuing legal education because of these instances of lawyer failure, hardly any of which are likely to be rectified by CLE.

Professional responsibility is clearly at issue when a lawyer fails to prepare adequately. However, that failure might be caused by a lack of common sense or judgment — two other lawyering skills that law schools can't teach — that can only be taught through on-the-job training.[9]

If I am correct that the major training failures in the American legal profession have been misunderstood by bar leaders, it should come as no surprise that the major institutions of the American bar have not adequately responded to the crisis in legal training. To be sure, lots of bustle has occurred: efforts to improve skills training in law schools through clinical education, experimental changes in the bar examination to test a larger range of skills, improvements in continuing legal education, mandatory continuing legal education, the certification of specialists, improvements in the disciplinary system, experiments in peer review, postgraduate skills training by such organizations as the National Institute for Trial Advocacy, in-house lawyer skills training programs, bar-sponsored mentor or buddy system programs, institutional efforts to help lawyers troubled by alcoholism and drug abuse, self-assessment programs modeled on the medical profession, and innovations in malpractice insurance.

But there is less to the lawyer competency movement than meets the eye. The profession is largely going through the motions because it has not yet perceived that lawyers need training in interpersonal skills so that they can relate better to clients and to other lawyers. Mandatory continuing legal education has been rejected by those truly concerned about lawyer competency. In the opinion of the lawyers who reviewed the concept in British Columbia, "The consensus is that mandatory CLE does nothing for the group of lawyers who are incompetent or close to incompetent."[10] Lawyers in Michigan, Massachusetts, Illinois, and other states have also rejected mandatory CLE proposals.

Law schools' efforts to expand skills training through clinical education have gone about as far as they can due to limited resources and resistance from tenured faculty, who believe that clinical instructors aren't sufficiently scholarly. And peer review is a nice concept that everybody talks about but that few are willing to act upon.

Supervision as an Ethical Obligation

Perhaps the most serious result of our neglect of interpersonal skills has been our irresponsibility in providing on-the-job training to the lawyers we supervise.

This has other implications but bears primarily on professional ethics. The importance of supervising lawyers was officially recognized for the first time in the Model Rules of Professional Conduct adopted by the American Bar Association in 1983.[11]

Although the ABA has been promulgating rules of conduct since the original Canons of Professional Ethics were adopted in 1908, the new Model Rules are the first to recognize a difference between the way law is practiced today and the way it was practiced in the eighteenth and nineteenth centuries. Until the ABA's latest effort, one could search in vain for any sign that lawyers practiced in firms, or that lawyers ever represented institutions more complex than the family farm. The image conjured up by previous canons of ethics was of the young John Adams, with a solo practice in Quincy, Massachusetts riding circuit, representing yeoman farmers and small merchants.

But read these excerpts from the new Model Rules:

RULE 1.1: COMPETENCE

A lawyer shall provide competent representation to a client. Competent representation requires the legal knowledge, skill, thoroughness and preparation reasonably necessary for the representation.

RULE 5.1: RESPONSIBILITIES OF A PARTNER OR SUPERVISORY LAWYER

(a) A partner in a law firm shall make reasonable efforts to ensure that the firm has in effect measures giving reasonable assurance that all lawyers in the firm conform to the Rules of Professional Conduct.

(b) A lawyer having direct supervisory authority over another lawyer shall make reasonable efforts to ensure that the other lawyer conforms to the Rules of Professional Conduct.

(c) A lawyer shall be responsible for another lawyer's violation of the Rules of Professional Conduct if:

(1) the lawyer orders or, with knowledge of the specific conduct, ratifies the conduct involved, or

(2) the lawyer is a partner in the law firm in which the other lawyer practices, or has direct supervisory authority over the other lawyer, and knows of the conduct at a time when its consequences can be avoided or mitigated but fails to take reasonable remedial action.

RULE 5.2: RESPONSIBILITIES OF A SUBORDINATE LAWYER

(a) A lawyer is bound by the Rules of Professional Conduct notwithstanding that the lawyer acted at the direction of another person...

Taken together, I read these provisions of the Model Rules to mean that:

(1) American lawyers have an ethical responsibility to practice competently;

(2) partners and other lawyers in supervisory roles have an ethical responsibility to see that their junior colleagues practice competently; and

(3) junior lawyers are not exonerated from ethical responsibility if supervising lawyers direct them to act other than competently.

Perhaps our supervisory responsibilities were always implicit in lawyers' professional ethics. But I find it refreshing to have them finally made explicit. And I find it especially noteworthy that lawyers' supervisory responsibilities should be set forth in rules of professional conduct at the same time in the history of our profession that we recognize the importance of interpersonal skills to the competent practice of law — skills that can hardly be taught in any other way than by supervision in the course of on-the-job training.

My reading of the new Model Rules, however, may go beyond what the drafters intended. There is only one explicit reference in the entire document to training or education, and that is in the Comment to the "competency" provision, Rule 1.1: "To maintain the requisite knowledge and skill, a lawyer should engage in continuing study and education. If a system of peer review has been established, the lawyer should consider making use of it in appropriate circumstances." The Comments to Rules 5.1 and 5.2 refer only to such classical ethical dilemmas as conflicts of interest and filing frivolous pleadings. I find no suggestion that the drafters thought about the relationship between Rules 5.1 and 5.2 on supervisory authority and Rule 1.1 on competence.

On-the-Job Training: Promise and Fulfillment

Lawyers should not wait for the ethical implications to be spelled out, however, before they act on their obligation to pass professional skills and knowledge from one generation to the next. Most law firms recruit new lawyers with the express or implicit promise that they will be developed and trained to their fullest potential. And if that potential turns out to be great enough, these recruits are led to expect that they will in some way become equity participants in the firm. In no other profession — not business management, not engineering, not accounting — are such extravagant promises made and so often kept. Even without an ethical code provision, this covenant imposes on us a serious moral obligation.

Lawyers Are Not Good Supervisors

The problem is that lawyers aren't very good at interpersonal relations, particularly at supervising younger lawyers or — if you will — conducting on-the-job training. Like the best scientists and scholars, the best lawyers are task-oriented, attacking and solving problems individually: they deliver case-by-case, matter-by-matter personal services to clients. Ironically, the reward for this kind of performance is seniority in an institution, usually a law firm, at which time lawyers are confronted with management tasks. Managers are not often judged on individual performance, such as the winning of a lawsuit or the negotiation of a business deal, but rather on their ability to manage other people who are responsible for the "line" work. In corporate institutions, managers don't do line work themselves but delegate and supervise it.

Ask the typical corporate manager what he does and he will describe his job in terms of supervising people and managing capital: "I am the vice-president in charge of the widget division. I have 3,000 employees under my supervision. My annual budget is $10 million and last year I reported a division profit of $1.3 million."

Ask a senior lawyer — even the managing partner of his firm   **9**

— what he does and he is more likely to say: "I'm a litigator." Or, "I'm a real estate lawyer."

It is mildly amusing — and vaguely heroic — that lawyers' supervisory responsibilities seem to be virtually invisible to them. Lawyers (like many of the best scientists and scholars) refuse to trade line responsibility for abstract management responsibility. Put another way, senior lawyers insist on remaining cowboys, even though others could ride the range, mend fences and rope steers, and the ranch desperately needs their services in the front office.

But the cowboy era has passed. Those cowboys who couldn't adapt to changing economics and technology were left behind. I do not suggest that the brave new world of legal practice is more romantic or more satisfying than the old world. But the new world is here, and those who resist it will be left behind as surely as the cowboy in the era of the feed lot.

The New Economics Requires Better On-the-Job Training

Although the economics of legal practice have changed dramatically in the past 20 years, lawyer development, or on-the-job training, has been one of the last areas of practice to be examined in light of new economic imperatives.

A number of related circumstances have affected the economics of law practice in the United States. In small firm practice involving mainly small business and personal law, the number of lawyers graduating from law school has increased enormously. While nobody knows precisely how many lawyers practice in the United States, the number may be as high as 600,000, and some project that we will have one million lawyers before the turn of the century.

It has now been almost a decade since the United States Supreme Court held that the Constitution prohibits the organized bar from forbidding lawyers to advertise.[12] Since that decision, lawyer advertising has become increasingly sophisticated. Such advertising has been notably successful in the service of national organizations providing standardized legal services at very competitive rates. Intense competition from these well-financed, well-managed, effectively-marketed legal service organizations, and more competition from the masses of new lawyers hanging out shingles as solo practitioners have required that solo and small firm practitioners manage their practices more efficiently.

Their first attempts to get organized included keeping careful time records, billing on a monthly basis, and paying attention to aging accounts receivable. But these lawyers soon discovered that better bookkeeping alone would not save them. The national legal service organizations, equipped with state-of-the-art technology and standardized operating procedures, checklists, forms, and precedents, could do the same legal work faster and cheaper.

So the next frontier in law office management was automation and standardization. Computers were purchased. Management consultants were retained. Yet somehow traditional practitioners found that they were still at a competitive disadvantage. Further investigation revealed that the highly efficient mass producers of legal services were better at hiring and training staff lawyers and paralegals.[13] Economic leverage was only partially a matter of better bookkeeping and higher technology. The fundamental secret was effective management of human resources.

Larger American law firms mainly representing institutions and wealthy individuals have been through management development stages similar to those of smaller firms. But the big firms have experienced additional problems that even more dramatically compel them to improve how they supervise and train their lawyers.

While the American economy has been down as well as up during the past twenty years, overall it has expanded enormously, causing a geometric increase in the demand for corporate legal services. Part of this demand has been met internally by corporations. In-house corporate legal departments have been created in many enterprises that previously relied exclusively on outside counsel, and have been substantially expanded and improved in others.

Firms specializing in corporate law have also expanded to meet the demand. Several now number over 350 lawyers; hundreds find themselves continuing to grow at an annual rate of 15 to 20 percent. To keep up with their work loads, these firms compete madly for law school graduates. And although the number of graduates has increased to over 30,000 per year, most of the competitive firms compete for the top ten percent of the graduating classes from the law schools with national reputations.

Thus successful students at renowned law schools find themselves with several offers, beginning with summer clerkships between their first and second years. They can be very fussy about where they take jobs. Starting salaries have been driven up to over $50,000 in the major metropolitan centers, and are not much lower in other cities where law firms need to bag their share of the best and the brightest.[14]

The overhead commitment represented by these new lawyers is enormous, and along with higher rents, support staff salaries, and the costs of state-of-the-art equipment have pressured firms to raise fees. At the same time, corporations have mounted a consumer revolution of sorts. Now that private firms are huge and costly to operate, they are insatiably hungry for business. Corporate general counsel are exploiting that hunger, refusing to allow any one firm to monopolize their business. They demand that law firms virtually bid on supplying legal services, much as other suppliers and contractors must bid competitively for the corporation's business.

So American law firms are caught in the classic cost-price squeeze. But there's an extra dimension to it. In a short-sighted belief that the only way to survive is to get the work out as fast as possible, senior lawyers have not given a high priority to on-the-job training of these highly paid new associates. This conscious decision to exploit associates from day one in the name of productivity conforms ominously with the fact mentioned earlier: lawyers are neither interested in nor trained to be good at interpersonal skills.

The result is disastrous. Senior lawyers fail to teach the skills that newer lawyers need to be excellent practitioners — the skills law schools do not teach. Young lawyers therefore never become as productive as they might be, and certainly not as proficient. These firms then are at a competitive disadvantage in bidding for legal work and may suffer a diminution in their profits. The young lawyers realize that they are not being adequately developed and their morale suffers. Productivity declines further. Ultimately they quit in favor of other firms where they will be trained more adequately, and where better management holds out a favorable prospect for personal growth, perhaps ultimately including an equity share in the firm.

Poor Training Leads to Unproductive, Unhappy Lawyers

This analysis depends to a large extent on my own experience as a consultant to law firms on lawyer training. But a recent survey sponsored by the Young Lawyers Division of the American Bar Association suggests that I am not seeing a skewed sample. In 1980, the Young Lawyers Division circulated an informal questionnaire to an unscientifically selected sample of lawyers under thirty-six years old. That survey indicated that fully 40 percent of the young lawyers responding were dissatisfied with their professional lives. To follow up, the Young Lawyers more recently undertook a comprehensive survey of lawyers randomly selected from ABA and non-ABA members: the National Survey of Career Satisfaction/Dissatisfaction.[15]

While the latest survey suggests that dissatisfaction is not as high as 40 percent, the results are still ominous for larger firms where young lawyers expect on-the-job training. In the latest survey, only 16 percent of all lawyers are dissatisfied, but the dissatisfaction level is 25 percent among junior associates and staff attorneys.

Many factors appear to affect job satisfaction, including firm size, the nature of the work assigned, intellectual challenge, and hours worked, but supervision is certainly among them. Forty-seven percent of junior associates were dissatisfied with the extent of supervision — whether defined as feedback on their work or the provision of instruction and training. Only 14 to 17 percent of junior associates reported frequent training and feedback from superiors.

The survey also supports my observations on the correlation between job satisfaction and law firm profits. In brief: "Dissatisfaction increases lawyer turnover and decreases lawyer productivity."[16]

According to the survey 25 percent of all lawyers plan to change jobs within the next two years; as a lawyer's dissatisfaction increases, the likelihood of his changing jobs increases dramatically. Even the 36 percent who scored "neutral" on the satisfaction scale plan to get a new job in the next two years. Nor does failure to advance in their present jobs account for the high rate of lawyers planning to switch jobs: only 16 percent of those in private practice report the reason for their proposed change as "limited or no advancement potential." Of those in private practice, 11 percent of partners, 26 percent of senior associates, and 35 percent of junior associates plan to change jobs within the next two years. This data confirms the information Joel Henning & Associates has collected during interviews with client firms. A remarkably high percentage of successful associates tell us that they do not want to be partners in the firms for which they work. In my view, this unhappiness with big firm practice stems from poor interpersonal relationships, including inadequate training, supervision, and mentoring.

The survey also attempted to measure "job strain." According to the survey framers, this item measures mental and physical strain, not specific illness, through a complex scale of items relating to depression, anxiety, psychological stress-induced physical illness, interpersonal problems, and obsessive/compulsive behavior. As one would expect, job dissatisfaction increases as job strain increases. But the strain level is extremely high — 66 percent — even for those who are neutral on overall job satisfaction, and is approximately as high for those who are somewhat dissatisfied. And 81 percent of those classified as very dissatisfied report that they are under high strain. These lawyers cannot be working up to their potential.

Lawyers Can Be Taught to Manage and Supervise

So. Interpersonal skills are important not only in practicing law but also in supervising younger lawyers in the course of on-the-job training. But law schools do not and likely cannot **13** teach these skills. Further, these skills do not come naturally to lawyers. Yet these skills are essential if firms — large and small — are to survive and prosper in the modern world. Without them, work cannot be efficiently produced and, ultimately, lawyers will despair and leave.

You could throw up your hands at this point and surrender. But surrender is not the only option: the requisite management and supervisory skills can be taught.

The skills ranked most important to the practice of law in the Bar Foundation study are:
(1) fact gathering,
(2) capacity to marshall facts and order them so that concepts can be applied,
(3) instilling others' confidence in you, and
(4) effective oral expression.

Law schools don't do a good job of teaching any of these skills, according to the lawyers surveyed. Nor did these lawyers believe that law schools were capable of teaching the second and third of them. To this list of skills lawyers desperately need but cannot get in law school I would add:
(5) common sense and good judgment, and
(6) the ability to manage and supervise the legal work of others.

If law school is not likely to do an adequate job of teaching these skills, neither is CLE, whether mandated or not. The answer lies within law firms themselves, which must impart these skills on the job. And it's worth noting that all of the others depend on a firm's ability to master the sixth skill. Without it, no progress can be made toward succeeding with the rest. If a law firm competing in the current economic climate is to survive and prosper, management and supervisory skills are desperately important. No amount of CLE seminars or formal in-house training programs can overcome senior lawyers' inadequate delegation, assignment, and supervision of day-to-day work. Most lawyers, however, admit that only a few of their colleagues devote the time and attention required to management and supervision.

Why is something so important so often done badly — or not at all? The first response one usually hears is that good supervision takes time, and today's competitive practice of law does not afford such time. But using time sheets, monthly billing, lawyer recruiting, and other aspects of law firm management also take time. Each of these time-consuming practices has gradually become an essential component of a lawyer's professional responsibilities. But until recently, only a few firms have expressly recognized that time devoted to supervision is at least as important as time committed to these other management responsibilities. In the rest of this chapter, I'd like to lay out some of the issues and techniques that we usually raise with law firm partners to help them conceptualize their on-the-job training responsibilities and improve their ability to carry them out. Later in the book I will expand on them.

The "I Can Do It Better Myself" Syndrome

Of course, an experienced lawyer can do almost any given legal task better than a tyro. But a senior lawyer also can, and should, do other, more important things that the tyro can't. Moreover, the tyro will never learn how to practice law if the senior lawyers always do everything themselves. In every American firm I have visited — without exception — partners too often draft simple pleadings, contracts, wills, briefs, and the like, when they should be establishing strategy, planning and budgeting cases, reinforcing client relations, managing the law firm, and seeking more clients.

Lawyers practice in firms to ensure that work is done at a high level of quality and is also done efficiently. Yet too many lawyers continue to act like independent feudal barons, having only tenuous relations with one another and little faith in delegating work. The fact is that work is efficiently performed when it is assigned to the lowest possible level in the firm; thus the quality of a law firm's work is not a function of who does it but who supervises it. A good manager (the antithesis of a feudal baron) knows how to delegate and how to supervise work. A poor manager tries to do it all himself.

The "Path of Least Resistance" Syndrome

Lawyers who do not insist on doing junior-level work themselves often fail as supervisors by *always* delegating work to experienced subordinates who know how to do it already. On the face of it this appears to be efficient because the work is channeled to those who can most easily get it done, along the path of least resistance. But if the same assignments are constantly made to the trusted aide who can carry them out with no supervision, that aide's development will be unfairly limited. He or she will get little or no new and challenging work. Also, the next generation of lawyers will be denied its opportunity to learn how to do the work monopolized by the trusted senior associate. Law firms that suffer from this syndrome discover fifth-year associates doing second-year work, a highly unproductive situation both economically and developmentally.

I venture that much of the unhappiness and compulsion to change jobs reflected in the Young Lawyers survey could be traced to poor work delegation. These problems are psychologically stultifying for young lawyers, and young lawyers who feel psychologically stultified tend to leave the firm, often before it can recoup its investment in their recruitment and training.

The Three Modes of Learning

Of course, once the work has been creatively assigned, on-the-job training is not over. As Mortimer Adler reminded us in his recent critique of American public education, *The Paideia Proposal*, people (including lawyers) improve their minds in three different ways: by the acquisition of organized knowledge, the development of intellectual skills, and the enlargement of understanding, insight, and common sense.[17]

Each of these learning modes demands different teaching techniques. Lawyers can pick up organized knowledge relatively easily, through textbooks, legal encyclopedias, forms, advance sheets, and CLE seminars. Law schools also teach this type of knowledge pretty well. On-the-job training does not duplicate or substitute for any of these useful and conventional modes of learning (except that experienced lawyers can and should help younger lawyers find the right books, forms, advance sheets, and CLE courses).

The supervisor and mentor should focus on the second and third modes of learning — skills development and sharpening judgment and common sense. Lectures won't do much to develop the skills lawyers identify as most important, such as fact gathering, marshalling and ordering facts so that concepts can be applied, instilling others' confidence in you, expressing oneself well orally, negotiating, and drafting legal documents. But on-the-job coaching and supervising will. Every time a lawyer personally rewrites an associate's draft and sends it out of the office without offering feedback to the draftsperson, that lawyer is abandoning his or her professional responsibilities as a supervisor. Similarly, denying junior lawyers the opportunity to observe negotiations merely because the firm cannot justify 100 percent billing for the extra lawyer on the scene is an abrogation of professional responsibility as well as a long-term handicap to the productivity of the junior lawyer.

That leaves open the question of how on-the-job training can teach young lawyers good judgment, insight, and common sense. Adler says that these elusive qualities of mind can be taught through dialogue and discussion. In the context of lawyer training, such dialogue and discussion are most effective as feedback delivered by the senior lawyer immediately after the junior lawyer has performed a significant professional task.

The question remains, though, how enlightened lawyers can convince their colleagues that time devoted to on-the-job training is not wasted, even though it means fewer hours to be billed to the client. The job of advocating adequate on-the-job training is not easy. However, such skeptical partners are not only wrong, they could lead their firms to extinction.

On-the-Job Training Makes Economic Sense

Every lawyer could be described as a profit center in cost-accounting terms. Until recently, one could easily argue that the lawyer who billed the most hours was the most profitable. That was because most legal matters were billed on a kind of "cost-plus" billing system. If the general counsel of ABC corporation, for example, hired outside counsel to try a case, or close a deal, the firm billed at a rate that met overhead and assured a handsome profit. Thus the cost-plus system typically allowed the firm to pass on the cost of its inefficiencies to the ABC corporation.

But corporations and even individual clients now understand that they can purchase legal services much as they purchase other goods and services, by scouting out the best product at the lowest price. In other words, in the modern era a firm pays for its own inefficiencies.

And an untrained associate is an inefficient lawyer. He or she, because of the nature of current legal education, comes to the firm without the skills practicing lawyers consider most important. If the associate is not trained within the firm, morale suffers, as the Young Lawyers survey indicates, and associates become even less productive, or even leave the firm.

Thus a firm's failure to invest in supervision and training will come back to haunt it when the new economics reaches its market. From that point on, profitability will not be correlated only with hours billed, but rather with delivering the best product, in the most efficient way, at the lowest cost. Although the time spent coaching and supervising cannot always be directly billed (though much of it legitimately can), that time will be rewarded when the supervisee becomes a more efficient lawyer or, in cost-accounting parlance, a profit center.

Every Lawyer Must Be Responsible for Training Junior Lawyers

The inescapable conclusion is that every lawyer must be individually responsible for the training of junior lawyers under his supervision. Law schools and continuing legal education can do much but they can't do what needs to be done. As the new Model Rules indicate, supervising junior lawyers is an ethical obligation. But ethics aside, the practice of law will be more profitable for those firms that effectively train their own lawyers. Thus on-the-job training is one of those rare responsibilities where our interest in doing good is reinforced by our obsession with doing well.

NOTES

1. Burger, *The Special Skills of Advocacy: Are Specialized Training and Certification of Advocates Essential to Our System of Justice?* 42 Fordham L. Rev. 227 (1973).

2. Bok, *A Flawed System of Law Practice and Training, Report to Harvard Overseers for 1981-82,* reprinted in J. Legal Educ. 570, 582 (1983).

3. *See, e.g.,* Toll, *A Modest Suggestion for Chief Justice Burger,* 66 A.B.A. J. 816 (1980).

4. *Giamatti Gives Notice, and Some Choice Observations,* N.Y. Times, April 28, 1985, E at 9.

5. F. Zemans & V. Rosenblum, *The Making of a Public Profession* (1981).

6. *Ibid.* at 142.

7. *Ibid.* at 139.

8. Report and Tentative Recommendations of the Committee to Consider Standards for Admission to Practice in the Federal Courts to the Judicial Conference of the United States 6 (1978).

9. Boudin, *Common Sense in Law Practice (Or, Was John Brown a Man of Sound Judgment?),* Harvard Law School Bulletin, Spring 1983.

10. Law Society of British Columbia, 1982.

11. Model Rules of Professional Conduct (as amended) 15 *et seq.* (1984).

12. *Bates v. State Bar,* 433 U.S. 350 (1977).

13. *The Fastest Growing Law Firm Employs 'Client Conscious' Training,* Lawyer Hiring & Training Report, Nov. 1984, at 1.

14. In the past couple of years, law school applications have declined 20 percent or more and are likely to continue declining. It's too early to tell what impact this decreased enrollment law schools will have on major law firm recruitment. One thing is certain. It will not expand the already small pool of law graduates "qualified" for large firm "elite" practice. See *Decline in Law School Enrollment Will Affect Law Firm Recruiting,* Lawyer Hiring & Training Report, May 1985, at 20.

15. Hirsh, *Are You On Target,* 12 Barrister 17 (1985).

16. *Ibid.* at 49.

17. M. Adler, *The Paideia Proposal* (1982).

Are Law Schools Losing Their Sense of Direction?

Why should a book on lawyer training bother about current problems in law school education? Because at least since the turn of the century legal practitioners and academics have argued about their respective responsibilities for training the next generation. The resulting confusions throw some light on the overall problem of lawyer training.

It may be unavoidable, but the law school curriculum could be driving misfits into your firm. Has it occurred to you lately that at least some of your recruits are not interested in long-term careers with your firm? Instead, they seek postgraduate skills training to become competent lawyers, and they know that the private corporate law firm is the best place to acquire that training. In a 1982 report, the Harvard Committee on Education, Planning and Development, chaired by Professor Frank Michaelman, found that 90 percent of Harvard Law School graduates went into private corporate law practice. "Remarkable and troubling," they concluded.

If you're skeptical that 90 percent want to be corporate lawyers, the facts bear you out. San Francisco's Brobeck, Phleger & Harrison reports that close to half of the associates who didn't make it in that firm had excellent academic records but never adjusted to the pressures of corporate practice. Also, they were not "team players" and often had personality conflicts with others in the firm, according to Gail Hewson, Brobeck's coordinator of professional activities.

My guess is that a substantial part of that 90 percent, including those who fit the Brobeck, Phleger "failure" profile, were after postgraduate training rather than partnership. If I am right, it tells us something worth knowing about law school education and about the need to refine your recruitment and hiring practices.

I am not suggesting that law school education be nothing more than Hessian training. But law professors now appear on the one hand to hold out law firm "residencies" as the only means to gain practical experience (and pay off law school tuition debts), while on the other they scorn corporate practice. Stanford Dean John Hart Ely was quoted in *The New York Times* as saying, "Frankly, deep down, most of the faculty don't have a lot of respect for [corporate law] as a career choice. I don't think that what corporate lawyers do is evil, but I myself would be uncomfortable working for a large firm. I wouldn't want to feel I was just a cog in a big machine."

If the law school experience isn't all it might be for your recruits, it may be that students themselves view law school differently than they used to. In the same article in which Dean Ely scorns corporate practice, Mark Kelman of the Stanford faculty dumps on law students: "For most students, nothing that goes on in law school matters — it's simply a credential . . . The most common student here is getting none of the real new clinical training, none of the new, financially sophisticated courses, no law and economics, no nothing. What this place offers is a ritzy degree, and there's a legal requirement that you spend three years here to get it." Kelman's comments are borne out by my own conversations with professors and students at major law schools.

There was a time when law students plunged head-first into their studies — at least for a year or two. Legendary law professors were strong, permanent role models for their students. That time was not so long ago. *One L*, the diary of Scott Turow, covered his first year at Harvard, 1975-76. Turow recalled in a recent conversation that: "at that time it was kind of a sub-rosa thing for people to get summer jobs after first year. The faculty frowned on it and it was not an approved part of the Harvard Law School program."

But the situation has changed. Students' interests go way beyond the institution. It's the old "how you gonna keep 'em down on the farm after they've seen Paree" problem. Large numbers of first-year students are offered interesting summer clerkships, for substantial sums of money, in private law firms. As Harvard Professor Arthur Miller put it: "The study of conflicts seems irrelevant after a summer spent working on a major corporate takeover."

20   Where is the incentive for total immersion in the law school

experience? And if hiring decisions are made in significant part before a student has passed through most of the curriculum, why should he or she strive mightily to succeed? Law firm policy and law school curricula are thus at odds.

In 1982, the power and attraction of the law firm recruiting game were set against Harvard's Olympian mindset: the law school attempted to shorten the recruiting season in order to minimize disruption to its class schedule. It soon discovered that many law firms and students either ignored or circumvented the Harvard edicts and has since backed down.

Let's face it, law schools cannot ever relate their courses to specific lawyering jobs. Nor can classroom instruction ever cover the process of employment, salary increases, specialization, and the partnership track, all of which are central to the world of private corporate firms. No wonder, then, that law students lose interest in their studies after one or two summers in the "real world." Even the law review experience suffers as a result. In a recent issue of the *Harvard Law Record*, Bob Riggle wrote about his Harvard Law Review experience: "Let there be no mistake, the Review's editors are not insensitive, uninspired, and downright boring, but the Review is."

The allure of early recruiting, and the correspondingly diminished attraction of law school classes, perhaps help to explain the next act in Harvard's modern soap opera, which was staged in the 1982-83 academic year. It began with a faculty debate on whether professors can, if they wish, consider classroom participation when deciding students' grades. A student's willingness to prepare for and participate in class could rationally be said to bear upon his or her ability to perform as a lawyer.

Harvard students favored what they called the "no-hassle pass." The students argued not only that professors should be forbidden to consider classroom participation in grading, but that they should also cease hassling students who refused to participate. Allowing professors to assign grades based on participation would make it easy, students said, for professors to discriminate.

Hassling (as oppposed to sanctions) was defined by the faculty as: "Suasion and encouragement to chastisement and display of displeasure... The instructor may address... comments specifically to the student who declined to participate; may continue to press that student for a response to the original question or a new or reformulated question for a response, on the ground that the student has a duty to try and respond, or that the question really isn't that hard to tackle, or that even error illuminates, or whatever; may assert that the student is in default of his or her responsibilities, that the student should try harder, that the student should see the instructor afterwards, or whatever." I particularly like the "or whatevers." Perhaps students who so violently oppose hassling imagine that it incorporates the use of cattle prods, Chinese water torture, hanging by thumbs, and breaking kneecaps.

Hordes of students, estimated at between 400 and 600, stormed Dean James Vorenberg's office after the faculty rejected both the no-hassle and no-sanctions pass (a move that left the question of sanctions where it had always been — with individual professors). This was the first time since Vietnam that more than a handful of students were mustered on behalf of any cause. Nobody quite knows how that many students wedged themselves into Vorenberg's office, but there they were. The faculty capitulated: realizing that it was not strong enough to resist, it was also too deeply divided ideologically, disagreeing on the origins, the nature, and the legitimacy of the students' concerns. As of today, Harvard professors may hassle but not sanction.

So once again, Harvard retreated. That's too bad because it was on the right track when it attempted to compress the recruiting season and when it resisted the no-sanctions and no-hassle pass. Harvard failed because it was out of touch with its constituencies — law firms and law students. It wasn't sensitive to the realities and constraints of their actions.

I don't intend to suggest, however, that law student ennui is exclusively the fault of law firms' premature and aggressive recruitment. Law professors must share responsibility. My alma mater, Harvard, is no exception. To be sure, Harvard is to some extent anomalous. With more than 1,700 full-time J.D. candidates, it is significantly bigger than most other law schools (Stanford, by contrast, has fewer than 550). Harvard's faculty numbers a whopping seventy professors. And its resources, combined with its celebrated (I am tempted to say fabled) name, enable it to do things that other schools only think of wistfully.

Nevertheless, since Harvard is my alma mater, I feel most comfortable — and justified — in criticizing it. Those seventy Harvard professors are extremely independent and willful. Many are also famous. But unlike former Harvard professors like Ames, Langdell, Pound, Scott, Hart, and Chadbourn, who were famous for being law professors, many at Harvard today are famous for other reasons. A few, I fear, are famous for being famous. As one faculty member put it, "publish or perish" has been replaced by "publicity or perish." Without denigrating the talents of this new breed of faculty, it's clear that many exploit their tenure at Harvard, or elsewhere, to pursue consulting fees and royalties, much as law students exploit these institutions to land high-paying jobs fast.

The Michaelman report came out in favor of more clinical education. But that parade has gone by. Every law school has some kind of clinical program, but some schools are discovering that the financial cost of meeting student demands for clinical education cannot be supported as enrollments level off. Moreover, student interest in doing good is being replaced by an obsession with doing well. To their wry amusement, administrators of these schools have also discovered that the very law firms that cried out for more practical teaching discount clinical courses on job candidates' law school records.

Other schools, including New York University Law School, have gone way beyond the threshhold questions on clinical education and are now asking how best to integrate practical problem solving into the law school curriculum. Some schools have built entire curricula around clinical experience, including Antioch School of Law in Washington, D.C., and the new Queens College Law School of the City University of New York. Queens, which admitted its first class of students in the fall of 1983, is doing well. Antioch, though, is facing disaccreditation by the American Bar Association and extinction.

Even so, we should moderate our expectations about improved lawyer training in law school. Since the days of Ames and Langdell, law school professors have prided themselves on being true scholars, part of the university community of scholars. That's one of the arguments used to bar clinical teachers from the tenure track.

Furthermore, today law schools are not on the cutting edge of many legal specialties. Most breakthroughs in fields such as tax, corporate law, bankruptcy, and matrimonial law, for example, are accomplished by practitioners serving clients, not by scholars living the life of the mind. Perhaps the best thinking on basic legal subjects, such as contracts, torts, and property, remains in the law schools, but those subjects are not where the action is in the profession. There are conspicuous exceptions, of course, like Louis Loss's work in securities law.

On the other hand, law firms don't have the time, nor do most lawyers have the temperament, to test ideas, reflect on deeper meanings, and weigh alternative conclusions. Nor does the hurly-burly of professional practice leave much time to consider ethical questions and human problems in the law. These are appropriate subjects for research by professors and study by students. Unfortunately, as this review of the Harvard scene suggests, these subjects seem to interest professors and students as little as they do practitioners in the trenches.

Socrates, Isaac Stern, and Nadia Boulanger: Legal Education Beyond the J.D.

Developments in the field of continuing legal education have been astonishingly diverse. Conventional CLE seminars proliferate, provided by commercial sponsors as well as bar organizations and law schools. The "CLE Calendar" in our monthly newsletter, *Lawyer Hiring & Training Report*, can give you a sense of the variety and depth — and shallowness — of conventional CLE offerings. New technology is being employed. Irving Younger's inimitable combination of Oliver Wendell Holmes and Sammy Davis, Jr. has been bounced off satellites into scores of cities and towns.

More than a dozen states mandate that all lawyers present their bodies at CLE seminars for a nominal number of hours, with no necessary correlation between the substance of the lawyers' practice and the subject of the CLE programs they choose to attend. A distinguished professor — an insurance law specialist — travelled to his state of licensure to attend a course in criminal law on the deadline — a complete waste of time and money, no doubt repeated often by other lawyers.

A few states require CLE of lawyers who have either designated themselves or been certified as specialists after fulfilling a series of highly controversial requirements. The oldest and probably the best of these plans, in California, is under constant attack from thoughtful elements of the organized bar and may be scrapped.

In this chapter, I want to focus on one aspect of lawyer training: the movement to train lawyers in practical skills and to undertake this training in the firms, corporate legal departments, and government agencies where these lawyers work.

Throughout this century, law schools have been troubled about their aims and methods. I have heard nothing lately to suggest that law schools are less troubled today. Instead, law firms and other organizations employing lawyers are beginning to question their old methods of making competent lawyers out of intelligent law graduates.

More than half our lawyers will never be employed by an entity with the time and resources to offer systematic training. According to a study published by the American Bar Foundation, though, 20 percent of private practitioners are in firms of ten or more, another 13 percent of the total lawyer population work for government agencies, and around four percent work for the Fortune 500 corporations. This means that well over one-third of the practicing bar is employed in organizations that probably do have the critical mass to do some training of their own lawyers. So I cannot be accused of focusing on an insignificant portion of the profession when I talk about in-house training.

According to the same ABF study, about 47 percent of lawyers are solo practitioners and one-third are in firms of fewer than ten. The ABA and a few enlightened state and local CLE organizations are attempting to provide the skills training for these lawyers. Their efforts remain in the developmental stage until the problems of curriculum, money, and administration can be solved.

One-third of lawyers in organizations capable of providing in-house training are likely to be exposed to it in the next few years if they have not been already. Some of the existing programs resemble law school clinical programs. At Heller, Ehrman, White & McAuliffe in San Francisco, a lawyer spends all of his or her time administering hundreds of small cases and counseling new associates who manage and try them. Unlike the typical law school clinic, this program includes cases that may be small but are in the mainstream of Heller, Ehrman's practice and its clients' businesses. Other firms offer comprehensive skills training programs like the one at Shearman & Sterling, covering everything from writing and editing to library research skills.

Small firms, as well as large model trial practice exercises after the excellent National Institute of Trial Advocacy. Baker & McKenzie was the first to retain a full-time director to establish a world-wide training program for its lawyers. Several others have now followed suit. Pitney, Hardin, Kipp & Szuch, one of New Jersey's largest firms, offers a full menu of skills training, including writing, negotiating, and deposition skills.

Our own evidence, gathered in publishing the *Lawyer Hiring & Training Report* and in providing training services to law firms, supports Zemans and Rosenblum's finding that "it is the neglect of competencies outside the law schools' self-defined mission with which practitioners find most fault," namely such skills as drafting legal documents (50 percent), other writing (nine percent), interviewing (11 percent), and negotiating (12 percent). Along with trial skills, these are the very areas that law firms are beginning to emphasize.

Why now? If this is such a good idea and so consistent with the weaknesses of the law school curriculum, why has it been so long in coming?

There are, I think, several reasons. First, many still believe that young associates learn practice skills by being apprenticed to senior lawyers. If this mentor system ever worked, it is hardly likely to work today. At $40,000 to $50,000 per year and more, a law firm wants to "eat" as few of a new associate's hours as possible. The pace of modern practice and the rapidly expanding size of corporate firms and legal departments also have made it unlikely that new lawyers will slowly and deliberately be brought along by older ones in the ordinary course of practice. Too many younger partners and senior associates are themselves caught in the frenzy of "making it" to have the time or the disposition to bestow their craft, if they have any, on the next generation.

Second, many lawyers remain skeptical that practical lawyering skills can be taught rather than assimilated.

Third, unlike corporations where management training is pervasive, law firms are not true hierarchies as defined by Max Weber and other sociologists. In the typical hierarchy, authority is organized in pyramid style: each official has authority over those under him. Anybody who has experienced a typical law firm partnership meeting can only be amused by the notion that a law firm is *any* kind of organized enterprise. Most make the Democratic Party look like a tightly disciplined organization. Most are collections of feudal barons: fiercely independent, arrogant, idiosyncratic, and often at war with one another.

These have been the obstacles to in-house training. It is now coming into its own for several reasons. The movement shows evidence of the growing concern — within and outside the bar — with lawyer competence. It is also in part an attempt by some firms to gain an edge in the zany recruiting game. And the law firm is gradually being modernized — or corporatized. More fims today operate on budgets, under relatively modern management, with an eye on productivity and efficiency. For example, a lawyer who can be trained to write and edit better and faster will be a more productive lawyer. But the main reason in-house training is now developing is the availability of: 1) demonstrably effective training methods; 2) trained outside instructors; 3) assistance in planning; and 4) assistance in training senior firm lawyers to teach skills. The programs are relatively efficient and relatively cost-free to clients whose matters need not be handled by young lawyers untutored by simulations and demonstrations. My experience in teaching these skills and observing others teach them is that the learning curve is surprisingly steep in most instances. Lawyers who do not catch on pretty quickly perhaps ought to practice in areas not demanding the skills they can't seem to master.

Although it is not a panacea for the bar's competency problems, in-house training may well take the heat off law schools to do everything they now do *and* turn out competent practicing lawyers as well. The philosopher Morris Cohen was famous for teaching his students to think like philosophers, not unlike teaching law students how to think like lawyers. In fact, Oliver Wendell Holmes said that he envied students who could sit at Professor Cohen's feet. But others criticized Cohen for teaching only analytical skills by the Socratic method. Cohen answered: "You have heard how Hercules cleaned the Aegean stables. He took all the dirt and manure out and left them clean. You ask me, 'What did he leave in their stead?' I answer, 'Isn't it enough to have cleaned the stables?'"

Of course, a clean stable does not a Kentucky Derby winner make. That requires good training (as well as good breeding), and that training takes money, just as legal skills training does. I do not want to rehearse the money argument for limiting the law school role in skills training. We all know it well. There are other reasons why skills training is better done in the firm than in the law school: institutional constraints limit the quantity and quality of skills training that law schools can provide.

First, the standard mode of law teaching is the Socratic method applied to legal cases. This creates an environment hostile to effective skills training, and to recruiting and keeping the best skills trainers. Socrates believed that the underlying foundation of his method was spiritual love between student and teacher. But the Socratic method in law school can and often does result in browbeating, sarcasm, and indeed the total absence of affection between teacher and student. Combined with the inevitable power that any teacher has over students, the Socratic method can be used by professors to terrorize students and, later, by students to terrorize family, friends, and — more to the point — colleagues and clients. Even when the Socratic method is used the way its namesake intended, it is no good for imparting skills, where progress is measured by results, not by a facility in handling provocative, and unanswerable questions.

Second, the law school curriculum is largely based on appellate case opinions. Because court cases arise out of conflict, they too contribute to the relatively cold and adversarial nature of the law school environment.

A third reason that skills training has not wholly succeeded in law schools is the intense competition among students for grades and other academic honors, including law review. Similarly, students are questing for jobs almost from the moment they are admitted, and teachers are squabbling for recognition, status, and academic advancement. Only the rare teacher can transcend these conditions and offer students the support and confidence essential to effective skills training. (Of course, these rarities exist. You and I know them and have watched with awe as they bucked the system and did a marvelous teaching job. Two out of my own experience are Federal District Judge Robert Keeton, formerly of Harvard Law School, and Gary Bellow, who remains there.)

Fourth, the practice of law and the skills it requires change faster than law school curricula — even clinical curricula — can. Cases and problems used in law school clinics and skills courses are not likely to resemble the actual practice that graduates will undertake.

These are among the reasons why clinical education — for all the attention it has received in recent years — remains more or less an unfavored stepchild of the law school. It's not just the battle over money or the intransigence of the faculty hierarchy. Skills training just doesn't fit easily with the techniques, the content, and the reward system of the law school. Students cannot know what skills they will need most in practice, and clinical faculty cannot know the most appropriate contexts in which to teach them.

How does the law school environment affect the skills of new lawyers who come out of it? When we teach negotiation within firms to new lawyers, we can almost always predict that more than half seek information as if they were cross-examining hostile witnesses: they will refuse to establish human relationships with the other parties, they will often exceed their authority, and they will fail to strike bargains in easy matters when their instructions were that the clients desperately wanted the deals. In short, they seem to start out committed to an adversarial mode of practice, although most of a lawyer's job is to resolve or avoid conflicts. They seem to be trained to be deal-breakers, not deal-makers — one reason, incidentally, why the public does not love us lawyers.

Similarly, lawyers in our writing courses are reluctant to "open up" and allow us to help them. They must be convinced, often after several weeks, that they will not be evaluated by the firm on the basis of their performance in the writing program and that we will bolster, not batter, their fragile egos as we work with them on this most essential of legal skills.

How is the learning environment different within the firm? **29**

Obviously there is some competition, but the organization depends for its short- and long-term success on a high degree of cooperation. Training can focus precisely on the skills important to each organization. And — with or without outside assistance — practical training can be provided by the most highly skilled practitioners. And, if you will allow me, perhaps a tad of spiritual love can be reintroduced into the teacher/student relationship, as Socrates intended.

Role models for skills trainers will not necessarily be law professors or even lawyers. They may be performing artists. See, if you can, a film called *From Mao to Mozart*. It documents Isaac Stern's trip to China, where he both performed and taught master classes in violin. In one scene, he asks a teenage Chinese violinist to *sing* a passage from Mozart that she has just played. She does so, beautifully. He smiles and tells her it was wonderful. Then he picks up his own fiddle and says, "why didn't you *play* it that way . . . make it sing." He demonstrates. She tries it, he laughs, compliments her, then gives her a kiss. Not precisely how a great session in negotiating skills should proceed but enormously instructive because we are observing a man who is a master craftsman, who loves his craft, who loves to teach his craft, and who loves his students.

Nadia Boulanger was one of the great music teachers of this century. Like Isaac Stern she was also a great performer, the first woman to conduct the Paris Philharmonic, the Royal Philharmonic in London, the New York Philharmonic, the Boston Symphony Orchestra, and the Philadelphia Orchestra — all before World War II. She taught Aaron Copland, Roger Sessions, Walter Piston, Virgil Thomson, and many others, including Joe Raposo, who composed and conducted much of the early Muppets' music. Her success as a teacher came from her closeness to her students, her willingness to laugh with them, and to exhort them when they were low and still far from accomplished. One of her students wrote: "She seemed to know a student's own idiom before he knew it consciously himself and to know, before he did, what he could stretch himself to accomplish. Her quiet confidence in each of us enabled us continually to outdo ourselves."

What does this example mean for practical skills training in the law? I think that lawyers should be brought along much as performing artists are. Even some of the same techniques are applicable, such as simulated exercises, demonstrations by experts, the use of video to pinpoint performance strengths and weaknesses, and most important, a sense of professionalism, of support, of confidence, of encouragement, even of love — all things that tend to be shoved aside in the law school environment.

The law firm and similar organizations are far preferable

"studios" for teaching these skills. Even bar associations may be able to develop the appropriate atmosphere for training solo practitioners and others not in larger firms. If I am at all correct, the implications for training *young* lawyers are obvious.

But I hope that other important results may also be achieved. Lawyers (male lawyers, at least) tend to lose interest in the law just when they have it made. They divert themselves with bar activities, politics, gold, or sex. Their energies stray from the firm and from enrichment of the profession just when they are capable of making their maximum contribution. But perhaps lawyers can become like those distinguished doctors who combine practice, learning, and teaching throughout their entire careers.

I am not talking about teaching and learning current developments in the law. We all have our own ways of keeping up: CLE seminars, advance sheets, legal journals, client-related research. I am talking about lawyering skills parallel to conducting an orchestra or playing the violin: the skills that the public thinks we are taught before being licensed but that — until now — have not been taught systematically anywhere.

And if this movement prevails, the heat will be taken off law schools to do *everything* necessary to prepare students for the practice of law. Within the profession, experienced lawyers as well as new ones will benefit. Most important, the public will find better representation from a profession that is not only learned, but skilled.

Mandatory CLE: An Incompetent Solution to the Competency Problem

It was still dark when Professor Spencer Kimball headed his car north from the University of Chicago on a 100-mile, pre-dawn trek to Milwaukee. Kimball, a world-renowned authority on insurance regulation, is a faculty member of the University of Chicago Law School, former Director of the American Bar Foundation, and former Dean of the University of Wisconsin Law School. This insurance expert and academic superstar was on his way to Milwaukee to take a continuing legal education course in criminal law.

Criminal law does not much concern Kimball, but he was six hours shy of fulfilling his mandatory CLE requirement in order to be recertified to practice in Wisconsin, and the deadline was approaching. He had to find a program that would provide the requisite hours, and he had to find it quickly. Hence the pilgrimage to Milwaukee to learn more than he cared to know about criminal law.

No matter that Kimball has taught insurance regulation and testified as an expert witness all over the country and before legislative bodies throughout the world. His specialty is relatively arcane, especially in Wisconsin. Like every mandatory CLE requirement, Wisconsin's does not distinguish between specialists and generalists, any more than it does between the competent and the incompetent.

Sagas like Kimball's have destroyed Dalton Menhall's faith in mandatory CLE. He is currently the executive director of the New Jersey State Bar Association, and was a draftsman of the Wisconsin mandatory CLE rule while executive director of that

33

state's bar association. "It's a bureaucratic nightmare, and the wrong approach to the competency problem," he now says. "If we've got incompetent lawyers, let's purge them from the system, or develop strict competency requirements."

Some, like Menhall, may have changed their minds about mandatory CLE, but past ABA president David R. Brink of Minnesota supported it. In a January 1982 speech before the Association of Continuing Legal Education Administrators, Brink said, "The virtue of mandatory CLE is that those who should, but don't, take voluntary CLE are exposed to training along with those who would take it anyway." He went even further, saying, "If you need to, make mandatory CLE even more mandatory, with attendance checks or even minimal exams on the content."

The Minnesota Supreme Court was the first to adopt a mandatory rule, in 1975, on the motion of the state bar, with more than a little support from Brink. He thinks opposition to it has been "in the large part emotional and doctrinaire."

Mandatory CLE, after all, is seductive to bar association types. When South Carolina became the ninth state to adopt a mandatory CLE plan, the president of the state bar was moved to declare that the lawyers of South Carolina now constituted the "vanguard of Southern progressivism."

Membership in this vanguard requires the lawyers of South Carolina to register for 12 hours of CLE per year. Other states with mandatory programs (there are 16) demand up to 45 hours every three years, or an average of 15 hours annually. Virginia is considering a proposal that would require only eight hours. That's clock hours, incidentally, not academic credit hours. So no lawyer currently has to spend more than a day or two per year in a CLE course. Spencer Kimball's pilgrimage to Milwaukee aside, this is not very demanding, especially in light of a 1976 ALI-ABA survey which indicated that lawyers who voluntarily attend CLE (almost 80 percent of the practicing bar) average 24.5 hours a year.

But, say the enthusiasts, the mandatory rule captures the lawyers who do not voluntarily attend CLE. This argument fails to indicate what purpose is served by rounding up all lawyers for attendance at CLE courses, courses that are not necessarily correlated with their practice. As Professor Kimball can testify, an insurance expert can fulfill his requirement in criminal law; or a tax expert can do his full penance in admiralty.

The movement, obviously, is a reaction to charges of incompetence, and nobody doubts that large numbers of lawyers don't do well some of the things they are paid to do. But that hardly justifies compulsory CLE. Actuarial data concerning lawyers' malpractice indicates that most actionable incompetence arises from sloppy work habits, like blowing statutes of limitations and screwing up title searches. Disciplinary matters mostly involve fees, neglect, and conversion of client funds. Mandatory CLE cannot do much to eliminate these embarrassments, any more than it can sober up the lawyer-drunks, straighten out the junkies, or rejuvenate the senile. (Ironically the senile and others in practice more than 30 years are exempted from mandatory CLE in South Carolina.)

Even if conventional CLE could make a difference in the way lawyers perform, the nine to 15 hours required are peanuts. Certified specialists in family medical practice must take 300 hours of continuing medical education every six years, or an average of 50 per year. Texas mandates 16 hours of law-related study for all eighth-graders, more hours than any state requires of its lawyers. The state of Washington requires its general practitioners in medicine to take an average of 50 hours of continuing education annually, but asks only 15 of its lawyers. Is the law only 30 percent as learned a profession as medicine? The fact is that the 15-hour standard was imposed arbitrarily in Minnesota, and has been as arbitrarily applied in the other mandatory states.

Most CLE courses present lectures and panel discussions that explore current developments in the law. The good courses, like the nightly TV news, help the audience stay current. But nobody has suggested that failing to keep up is a serious problem among lawyers. Furthermore, just as the *New York Times* is an alternative to Ted Koppel, there are lots of other ways for lawyers to keep up. Why force this one on everybody, especially when it is costly not only in time lost from practice but in out-of-pocket expense?

Zealots insist that mandatory CLE insures a threshhold level of performance. But they have no proof. It is true that in Minnesota more than 80 percent of lawyers surveyed said that mandatory CLE improved their competence, but that is at best a bootstrap argument. No empirical studies have correlated CLE and lawyer performance. And the news from other professions is not promising. Several studies have failed to find a demonstrable relationship between doctor performance and participation in continuing medical education. In one study, the effect of routine continuing medical education programs was measured by examining the responses of doctors to unexpected abnormalities in laboratory tests. The performance of doctors who attended relevant continuing medical education seminars was not significantly better than that of their colleagues who did not attend. In fact, the American Medical Association recently wrote that "the justification for mandatory continuing medical education . . . probably does not stand up under close scrutiny. Enforcing such a requirement would not identify the small number of errant physicians within the medical profession." A

1977 National Science Foundation study of 2,500 engineers in six companies found no correlation between performance rankings and continuing education courses taken. Benjamin B. Wells, M.D., Director of CME at the University of Alabama, articulated the feelings of many doctors in his widely-reprinted 1976 paper, "The Case Against Mandatory CME":

> "...We have thus far found no way to demonstrate or measure improvements in the practice of medicine as a result of educational efforts. Moreover, we have yet to develop objective methods to determine educational needs among physicians... CME remains essentially experimental and pragmatic both in method and content."

Problems of lawyer competence transcend individual sloppiness, overreaching, and ill health. The Chief Justice, among many others, believes that the overall level of lawyering skills, especially courtroom skills, is dismally low. But conventional CLE courses cannot significantly improve a lawyer's *skills* any more than a Balanchine lecture might have made a ballet dancer out of an oaf.

The National Institute for Trial Advocacy offers only an apparent contradiction: this highly respected program has been evaluated and does appear to make trial lawyers better. But it bears no resemblance to typical CLE programs. NITA uses closely supervised simulations, employing a far lower ratio of students to faculty than usual in CLE courses. Furthermore the NITA program is three weeks long: students are in class 96 hours and actually work an average total of 180 hours. Variations on the NITA model have dramatically reduced the time involved, but even its condensed versions require a minimum commitment of many more hours than any of the mandatory programs.

Training in other lawyering skills also requires much more time than the mandatory rules stipulate. The ABA's course in "office" skills, including interviewing, counseling, negotiating, and drafting, demands approximately four times the hours required under the South Carolina mandatory rule. Joel Henning & Associates offers a lawyer's writing workshop that ideally involves approximately 20 hours of workshops and tutorials.

Instead of stimulating skills training, mandatory CLE has retarded it. In states with mandatory programs some CLE organizations have difficulty offering in-depth skills courses because of the relentless demands for enough conventional stuff to insure that the entire bar can get in its required hours. And then there's the question of money. These intensive courses, stretching over many days or weeks, with low teacher/student ratios and high administrative overhead, are substantially more expensive than a panel discussion in a hotel ballroom.

The argument of last resort in support of the mandatory CLE movement is that consumers and legislatures are casting a jaundiced eye on all the professions. However, it is difficult to see that mandatory CLE will offer them any reassurance: we can never prove to the world that mandatory CLE works, because the lawyer's obligation ends with his physical appearance at the site of the course. Without any testing mechanism, no one will ever know if he brought his mind along. Nor can we urge the public to have faith that quantity will produce quality, because our mandatory hourly requirements are significantly lower than those of other professions.

Many continuing legal educators have opposed mandatory schemes. They roundly condemn the concept at every opportunity. Their own association has never endorsed it. The not-for-profit providers have in fact suffered from the imposition of mandatory CLE: they have been required to churn out lots more programs, in some cases without significant increases in budget or staff. The occasional "blockbusters" that might bring in the revenues to underwrite less popular but equally important courses are now offered by commercial competitors, who take the money and run. CLE administrators have sometimes been put in an impossible position. In Washington, the CLE director for the state bar has also been saddled with responsibility for accrediting all CLE courses. In a classic conflict of interest, he submits courses for accreditation and then passes on his own courses as well as his competitors'. Worst of all, the time he spends on accreditation is time stolen from CLE planning, and vice versa.

Other efforts underway are more likely to reduce public skepticism about the legal profession. Some involve CLE requirements geared to lawyer performance. In California and Texas, lawyers wishing to be certified in certain specialties sit for a tough exam and then commit to annual CLE in their specialties. Self-designation plans, like Florida's, require CLE in the specialties the lawyer claims to possess.

Another effort involves some policing of the profession. To discourage financial hanky-panky, several states have initiated spot audits. All law firms can be, like banks, surprised at any time by an accountant authorized to review their books and records. Beefed-up disciplinary activities and peer review also are likely to improve lawyer performance.

Maybe some day mandatory CLE will be seen as the first tentative step toward upgrading the profession. If, however, these cosmetic mandatory CLE programs are deemed to put the legal profession in the "vanguard of progressivism," the search for truly effective means of improving lawyer performance may be slowed, if not abandoned.

The confusion over mandatory CLE reminds me of a scene in

Alice in Wonderland. Alice, lost, meets the Cheshire cat. "Would you tell me, please, which way I ought to walk from here?" she asks. "That depends a good deal on where you want to get to," answers the cat. The South Carolina Bar congratulated itself on getting to mandatory CLE. But as Spencer Kimball can tell them, they are confusing the means with the end. At best, CLE is a modest means toward the end of upgrading the competence of the profession. And we are a long way from getting to that end. CLE may have an important, if limited role to play, but mandatory CLE has none.

Getting Started
in Lawyer Training

Lawyer Recruitment and Training Are Two Sides of the Same Coin

A good in-house lawyer training program requires planning, budgeting, organizing, purchasing equipment, choosing specific skills to be addressed, finding appropriate trainers, and determining appropriate trainees. These might be called the "trees" of lawyer training.

But let's briefly step back and look at the forest: how lawyer training relates to entry level lawyer recruitment, lateral hires, automation, productivity, overhead, fees, budgeting, profitability, leveraging, administration, and management. To achieve this broader perspective, let's reflect on law firm rather than lawyer performance. When we examine law firm performance, we are likely to become more discriminating about lawyer training.

From this longer perspective, lawyer training appears poorly defined and troubled. It involves a jumble of purposes, instructors, materials, politics — bar politics and law firm politics — and economics.

Several influences shape — or distort — the design and content of lawyer training. First, there is public disillusionment with lawyers, and a brooding sense of trouble within the profession. This disillusionment stems in part from concerns about lawyer training before and during our careers and, ultimately, about our competence.

Second, we're witnessing a rise in legal specialization. Most of it is practical and informal, but some of it is official. California, Texas, Florida, and a few other states have created programs to designate or certify specialists.

41

Third, the law schools are confused about their appropriate role — especially the proper mix of scholarly and clinical education.

Fourth, the profession is experiencing tremendous growth and ferment. Not only has the absolute number of lawyers grown, but the size of some law firms and corporate legal departments has expanded almost exponentially. Multi-office national and international firms proliferate. This rapid growth has many implications, not least of which is a vitiation of the old relationships among lawyers, especially between senior lawyers and junior lawyers, masters and apprentices, or mentors and proteges. A new ABA Task Force is investigating the decline of professionalism.

A fifth concern, in part a result of these others, derives from the risks and costs of professional liability.

The last of the distorting influences, but perhaps most important, is the inflationary cost of everything, especially the cost of associates. Rising costs influence all aspects of legal practice, including lawyer training.

These distorting influences have produced much activity in the field of lawyer training. Unfortunately, a great deal of it is confused and some of it is downright hysterical. In some jurisdictions, the bar has adopted merely cosmetic gestures, such as mandatory continuing legal education. About 16 states now have mandatory CLE rules; Idaho and Nevada, for example, require bar members to attend ten hours of CLE each year. Virginia is considering a seven hour annual requirement. There may or may not be reasons for mandating continuing legal education, but if there are good reasons, surely seven hours a year is well below the threshold of meaningful attendance.

The movement for in-house training has been another focus of activity. Generally healthy, it is still subject to many of the same distorting influences as other forms of lawyer training. A firm management committee or an eccentric senior partner can get exercised over the need to provide a particular training program. Such "hot flashes" can be expensive and embarrassing. For example, some law firms have hired a woman who purports to teach "communication skills." I have heard her perform twice. She says that when you cross your arms you're using body language. She says if you wear red, you're sexy. She charges more than $1,000 for such insights. Henny Youngman may cost as much, but he's funnier and no less instructive. Or an occasional senior partner will insist, "The big problem with legal writing is that too many young lawyers begin sentences with prepositional phrases." I remind him of a sentence that began "In the beginning . . . ."

Some firms invest enormous amounts of money in excellent trial skills programs when most of their cases and their lawyers never go to trial. Such firms may do nothing to help lawyers improve discovery skills they use more often, and nothing to improve "office skills" like interviewing, counseling, and negotiating. Other firms may reject elaborate programs for associates, maintaining that their mentor systems are adequate. Yet most of these fail to help their senior lawyers improve their supervisory skills.

All firms must confront the tension between the need for lawyer training and the enormous pressure to keep costs and fees down. Lawyer training, like other elements in law firm overhead, ultimately finds its way into the fee structure.

Unless in-house lawyer training yields a substantial return on investment, lawyers can't afford such programs in an era of high costs and increasing client resistance to higher fees. The fundamental question then is not whether lawyers can learn something in a training program but whether that learning will make a difference in the quality of their practice. Studies in other professions reveal little or no correlation between conventional professional education and the quality of professional services. Doctors, for example, have not discovered a significant correlation between patient outcomes and continuing medical education.

It may be helpful to begin your plans for an in-house training program by asking: 1) Who are the successful lawyers in your firm? 2) What are their outstanding professional qualities? 3) How do these lawyers keep up with current developments in the law? (Many never attend a continuing legal education course.) The answers to these questions will provide you with a list of characteristics, some of which will relate to in-house training, some of which will relate to external continuing legal education, but many of which have nothing to do with training but rather with recruitment, library acquisitions, and firm management.

The rating sheets used by many firms to evaluate candidates for partner may be instructive. These typically list such attributes as writing ability, speaking ability, negotiating skills, potential for attracting new clients, ability and willingness to handle different kinds of work, ability to effectively supervise the work of others, ability to deal with clients, ability and willingness to handle a large volume of work, cooperation with other lawyers in the office, and overall capacity for continued professional growth.

You can train lawyers to develop some of these characteristics, but others fall to God, chance, recruiters, spouses, health, character, personality, and energy. For example, you may be making a serious mistake if you highly value the ability to deal with clients but limit your recruitment efforts to members of the Harvard Law Review.

Doctors in some clinics, along with their nurses, office managers, and accountants, occasionally sit down and ask themselves: 1) What are our biggest problems in patient care? 2) Which of these problems can be solved by changing conditions in our offices and our examining rooms? 3) Which can be solved by better supervision or mentoring? 4) Which can be solved by external continuing medical education? 5) Which can be solved by formal in-house training? 6) Which can be solved by better hiring and firing decisions, or earlier hiring and firing decisions? 7) Which have no solutions?

If lawyers follow this model, questions about training will boil down to questions about desired "client outcomes." And lawyers will see the links between recruitment, management, and training.

Training Your Firm's
Lawyers:
The Future Is Here

The days of training lawyers by osmosis are numbered. More and more law firms are discovering that on-the-job training, though important, is not sufficient to insure that associates quickly become productive. As a result, firms are initiating formal in-house training programs that cover everything from trial practice to the skills required by senior lawyers in on-the-job supervision of associates. They are overhauling their in-house systems of professional development, and the rest are likely to follow.

Until recently, many lawyers were unwilling to concede that their professional development required formal and systematic attention. Professional development was assumed to occur as new associates experienced the harsh realities of real-world lawyering, tempered under the "mentor" system by the wisdom and guidance of senior partners.

Why has the demand for in-house lawyer training grown so rapidly? There are several reasons, most of them related to sound law firm management in the competitive market for legal services.

Rapid law firm growth is an important factor. In the days of measured and stable growth, almost every new associate could be assigned to a single mentor or supervisor. In most firms, there were enough senior lawyers to go around, and each new associate could have a one-to-one relationship with an experienced lawyer. Today, junior associates outnumber the partners and senior associates available to supervise and train them. Junior associates thus may be assigned to work for other associates who are not much older or much more experienced. As a result, the quality of on-the-job supervision and mentoring may decline. In addition, a kind of intramural competition may affect the supervisory relationship. Placed in a supervisory position to ease the burden on partners, some senior associates subconsciously may assign younger associates to less meaningful work because they perceive the juniors as vying for the same limited number of partnership slots they themselves covet.

Law firm economics also play a role. Legal clients are in the vanguard of the consumer revolution. Even multinational corporate clients are demanding strict accounting from their lawyers and are not pleased to see on-the-job training time of young associates reflected in fee statements.

And just when clients began to demand that fees be contained, associate salaries escalated significantly. When law firms were paying associates $375 per month, partners could afford to be more relaxed about the pace at which associates became productive. They could bring associates along to observe trials, negotiations, depositions, and client interviews. But when associates are paid many times that amount and occupy extremely high rental space, partners justifiably demand a faster return on their investment.

The changing economics of law practice also have reduced traditional training opportunities. The rising costs of litigation have robbed many firms of the small cases that were wonderful on-the-job training devices. Formerly, these cases gave young litigators trial experience early in their careers; today, they are given few if any of their "own" cases. Instead, they are likely to be shunted to minor roles in complex litigation, far from the center of case planning and far from the courtroom.

The new economics also have dealt a heavy blow to the traditional "rotation" system. Until recently, new lawyers might have been exposed to several (if not all) of the firm's legal specialties or departments. Today, however, many law firms are abandoning rotation, and for good reason. Rotation frustrates partners because they lose young associates just as they begin to be useful. Associates are impatient with rotation because they are compelled to spin their wheels in several specialties before they can establish themselves within the firm's structure.

These economic factors mean problems for on-the-job training, problems that are aggravated by the accelerated pace of law practice. These days, senior as well as junior lawyers tend to work harder. When everybody is working as hard as they can to serve clients, little time remains for old-fashioned mentoring, supervision, and personal coaching.

The increased stakes in lawyer recruiting also have had an impact on in-house training. When new lawyers are deciding which offer to accept, they look for effective training programs, in part because the practice of law has become relatively unstable in the last few years. New lawyers know that they are unlikely to make partner in the firms where they hold their first jobs. As a result, new lawyers want to know how you, their employers, will train them not only to serve your needs, but to prepare for a career in the legal profession, in your firm or elsewhere.

And let's face it, your young lawyers are a new breed presenting new problems in training. Their values are different. They may be less willing than their predecessors to sacrifice their personal lives for professional success. Moreover, the modern law firm is more likely now to reflect the ethnic, religious, and racial character of the country than it was a generation ago. Perhaps the most striking change is in the growing number of women entering law firms, many of which currently hire as many women lawyers as men.

As a result, traditional modes of coaching young lawyers may not work. A recent study indicated that young female professionals may receive poorer training than their male counterparts. It was not that the women believed they were being discriminated against by reason of their sex, but that their male supervisors were uncomfortable with them. Consequently, supervisors were unable to provide feedback as easily to young women as to young male professionals.

The same kinds of problems strain communications between supervisors and supervisees who are members of different ethnic and racial groups. The traditional law firm could rely on an easy flow of communication among people from similar backgrounds and similar schools who had been socialized in similar ways. This can no longer be taken for granted.

Another strong reason for developing in-house training programs is the growing realization that law schools don't produce lawyers. Hardly anybody will argue today that a bright law graduate is competent to practice law without further training.

Law schools do reasonably well at preparing students intellectually and introducing them to traditional areas of substantive law. But law schools do not teach adequately the fundamental skills that lawyers use every day. These include effective oral expression in court and elsewhere, negotiating, client interviewing, writing and editing, the exercise of good judgment and common sense, the ability to work as part of a team, and the ability to attract and maintain clients.

There's a big difference between a textbook dilemma and a client with a problem. Many senior lawyers are frustrated by the inability of associates to go beyond issue spotting and intellectual analysis to resolve actual cases in a real — not an academic — setting.

In fact, the law firm may be the best place to teach lawyering skills. Clinical methods have been developed by practitioners working with law schools and organizations such as the National Institute for Trial Advocacy (NITA) and the American Bar Association Consortium for Professional Education. Law schools expanded their clinical programs in the '70s, but many law school deans, including Harvard's former dean Al Sacks, believe they do as much as they legitimately can. Their reluctance is in part philosophical and in part financial. Most law professors have limited practical experience and deeply believe in the case method. They argue that there is no telling in law school which skills any given student will need for his or her practice. Establishment professors tend to scorn clinical methods and clinical instructors. Most important, clinical-style teaching requires active participation of students and close supervision of faculty, which demands low student-faculty ratios. This inevitably means higher costs.

Nor does conventional continuing legal education meet all of the needs unmet by law schools. CLE is valuable, but it tends to cover current developments — much like the nightly news on television. Both keep the audience current and warn of impending disaster but hardly prepare them to take an active role. Even those who highly value CLE admit that it fails to adequately teach many of the lawyering skills central to successful law practice. Nor does CLE prepare young lawyers to serve the specialized, often highly technical needs of a particular firm's clients.

With the exception of a few organizations like NITA that specialize in clinical methods, CLE providers are even more reluctant than law schools to offer much skills training. Most CLE providers are comfortable with substantive law programs for which they need only choose among abundant speakers and book conventional sites. They perceive the administrative and pedagogical complexities of skills training in the clinical style as burdensome, and they are right. CLE providers also argue that they are in business to serve lawyers in volume, while clinical programs at best reach only a small number of students. The high cost of clinical programs is an even greater deterrent to CLE providers than to law schools, because the former, lacking endowments and alumni contributions, are limited to revenues earned from tuition.

In fact, the chief advantages of high quality external CLE seminars often are not educational. Instead they offer busy lawyers a change of pace and scenery. They may stimulate creative thinking and raise morale. They offer opportunities for specialists to meet and share ideas. And they can produce referrals.

The exigencies of the modern legal world have thus severely

limited the effectiveness of traditional training. Indeed, until recently most lawyers considered that lawyering skills were biologically acquired in a process not unlike the one in which a caterpillar metamorphoses into a butterfly. When skeptical lawyers discovered that many lawyering skills could be taught, the movement toward in-house training accelerated. Thanks to pioneer work by NITA and the American Bar Association, among others, effective materials and techniques are now available.

Today, law firms have a choice. They can assign their own lawyers to research, plan, and conduct an in-house training program, or they can bring in consultants to help in the planning and instructors to do some or all of the teaching. Some firms do it all themselves, others find it more cost-effective to use some outside experts as well as in-house resources.

In the law firm, if low student-faculty ratios are required, a program limited to five or six lawyers is no less cost-effective than one geared for many more students in a law school. And if the law school is an inappropriate forum to teach skills because students don't yet know what skills they need, the law firm is ideal. Each course can be tailored to suit the firm's specialized needs.

If law professors tend to lack practical experience, senior lawyers within the firm have it in abundance. Obviously every lawyer is not by nature a good teacher, but those with interest and aptitude can be trained in clinical methods in a short time. The challenge of helping to train the next generation may even reinvigorate bored lawyers.

The high cost of associates is a strong incentive to accelerate their professional development. Even if 80 percent of a lawyer's proficiency comes from experience and not from formal training, the incremental gain that might result from a formal program becomes economically significant to a firm that adjusts billing rates as its lawyers become more skillful.

In-house training programs based upon simulations can reduce the likelihood that inexperienced lawyers will develop bad habits and can help them shed any they might have acquired. More important, lawyers hone their skills in simulations without possible injury to clients.

Yet for all of its benefits, an effective professional development program in not easy to develop. In-house training works well at AT&T because it is a highly structured, tightly managed organization. While law office management has improved over the last decade, many firms remain collections of independent feudal barons who resent the imposition of form and structure. Busy, independent lawyers are not easily compelled to participate as students or teachers. If no more than the occasional partner will offer his or her time — or associates' time — for **49** training, the effort is doomed.

There are as many models for effective in-house lawyer training programs as there are law firms with such programs. After developing its in-house program over more than a decade, Shearman & Sterling hired a full-time director of CLE. Their choice was a professor of English with extensive administrative experience in the academic world. He and his successor administer all of Shearman & Sterling's training programs, as well as devote considerable time to the firm's legal writing and editing. Baker & McKenzie hired a law school professor as its full-time director of professional development. He was soon replaced — by another academic — and returned to the academy. Between them, they helped to develop an extensive program to serve Baker & McKenzie's many offices in this country and abroad. Los Angeles's Paul, Hastings, Janofsky & Walker hired an administrator with experience in adult education. She had not previously worked with lawyers. Other firms have redefined the role of their recruitment coordinators to include responsibilities in the lawyer training area.

Most firms, however, have not taken on full-time staff, but have created committees of lawyers to plan, budget, and oversee their in-house training efforts. The training committee works closely with the hiring and personnel committees but typically devotes its full attention to planning and implementing training programs for junior and senior lawyers. Often the committee also oversees external CLE attendance.

You want to know what constitutes a good in-house program. But don't, in your enthusiasm for developing one, ignore external CLE. Careful investment of lawyer time and firm money in external CLE is cost-effective. This doesn't mean sanctioning an unlimited budget for external CLE programs. CLE seminars should be carefully chosen. Lawyers attending should share notes and course materials with their colleagues during an in-house seminar, perhaps during lunch. (*Lawyer Hiring & Training Report*, our monthly newsletter, carries a CLE Calendar that can save you time in organizing the flood of CLE brochures that come across your desk.)

The birth of in-house CLE should not signal the death of CLE organizations. Most lawyers do not practice in firms large enough to justify in-house programs. Even large firms cannot efficiently produce some external offerings. The NITA program, for example, is more elaborate and probably better than any in-house advocacy program. Although Shearman & Sterling and Morrison & Foerster both have extensive advocacy programs in-house, they continue to send their most promising litigators to NITA for additional training.

Nor does it make sense for law firms to shunt senior lawyers from client matters into preparation of substantive law seminars that may be no better than those offered publicly. It is often vastly more expensive to prepare an in-house seminar than to send a few lawyers outside to a good program. Large CLE seminars on substantive law also provide a wider variety of ideas and viewpoints than are likely to arise in a program restricted to lawyers from any one firm.

Nonetheless, some subjects, writing for example, are almost impossible to teach except in-house. The challenge is to teach them well. Several firms have retained English professors with no sense of the law and how it is practiced. As a result, they often impose assignments on their lawyer-students that are rightly perceived as make-work. English professors are also stymied by lawyers' arguments defending stylistic atrocities alleged to be legal imperatives. Our consulting firm insists that lawyers who write well be included on any legal writing faculty. As a result, we often discover that "poor writing" is the result of vague work assignments, or inadequate research skills, or the idiosyncratic literary expectations of senior partners.

Video recording and playback equipment is a useful tool in a comprehensive in-house training program, but in-house training is not necessarily synonymous with a massive and immediate investment in equipment. Many firms have made the mistake of equating the purchase of hardware and a few videotaped CLE programs with the successful development of in-house training. As a result, the equipment gathers dust in a storage closet or a corner of the library, and the videotaped CLE programs are never seen by lawyers who might be helped by them.

The effective use of video begins with a careful screening of available CLE videotapes. Once you've got them, rarely, if ever, should you expect a lawyer to sit down alone to watch one. However, the best CLE videotapes can be effective in-house training tools when they are integrated with a live in-house training program conducted by you or your colleagues. Video is a passive medium. To make it into an active teaching tool, you must bring the session to life by prompting dialogue and debate among all present.

The most exciting use of video for lawyer training is as a "mirror." Lawyering skills such as trial practice, negotiating, and client interviewing and counseling are most effectively taught through simulations. Lawyers, like all human beings, survive partly through denial. But when a video camera has recorded a lawyer's "performance," he or she can hardly deny what has occurred. Instead, steps can be quickly taken to correct the problems. The learning curve is extremely abrupt when you effectively use clinical-style simulations supported by videotape recording and playback.

The best in-house programs do not require great expense but **51** desperately need careful planning. Firms that have been most successful don't try to spoon-feed their associates with costly programs in a futile attempt to meet every need unmet by the law schools. Young lawyers are not helpless infants but professionals who remain ultimately responsible for their own professional development. And they will appreciate any effort you make toward tailoring a program to their specific needs.

So, before announcing any workshops or seminars, the training committee should spend considerable time creating a plan for its lawyer development program. The first step is to inventory the skills your firm depends on today and is likely to need in the future. The next step is to map out the progress you expect of your associates in acquiring these skills. For example, what skills should a corporate lawyer have achieved at the end of one year of practice? Two years? Five years? What skills must he or she have mastered before a partnership offer is likely to be made?

Once your firm has carefully developed its career profiles or "roadmaps" of successful lawyering, you can decide what training resources to make available within the firm to help achieve those goals. You will be able to prepare a careful budget to meet your actual training needs, not your fantasy training desires. Many firms, for example, focused their early in-house training efforts almost exclusively on trial skills. But after careful investigation, these firms discovered that associates were being trained at enormous expense in trial skills that they only rarely (if ever) used. On the other hand, these associates were frequently thrown into pretrial practice, discovery (including depositions), and negotiation of settlements, with virtually no training or experience.

So early concentration on trial skills training has been replaced by more broadly based programs that include such pretrial skills as motion and discovery practice. All lawyers, including those who deal exclusively with corporate, tax, real estate, and probate matters, are being trained in legal writing and editing, negotiating, client counseling, and practice management. Nor do training programs consist only of elaborate clinical-style skills workshops. Many litigation, corporate, and real estate departments have developed useful training programs around their forms and checklists: a lawyer may be assigned to review an important form or checklist, or to develop a new one; then all lawyers in the department participate in refining it.

Once you have established your needs and set goals, you will discover that a good training program yields side benefits. First, your needs inventory can improve your recruiting practices and rationalize the process by which you evaluate associates.

Second, you will discover that some of the attributes you want to develop in your lawyers are not so much technical skills as matters of judgment, clear thinking, and common sense. We tend to think that these qualities come with experience, but they can be nurtured through training programs. Senior lawyers can't necessarily "teach" judgment and common sense to associates, but they can demonstrate them through their responses to questions and other informal interactions. Previously this teaching by example would have occurred naturally in the course of supervising legal work. It still should and must. But the modern law firm doesn't have enough good supervisors who have enough time to do all that should be done.

You also will discover that a good training program is by no means limited to new lawyers: virtually all successful in-house programs include workshops for senior lawyers as well. Senior lawyers, for example, spend a great deal of time editing preliminary drafts by junior lawyers. Few, however, can edit efficiently or explain their edits to younger draftsmen. As a result, senior lawyers spend too much time rewriting and too little time improving young lawyers' skills. In addition, the programs available to help partners become better editors and writing coaches offer more "bang for the buck" than those aimed only at junior lawyers. Not only is there less turnover among senior lawyers, but more important, senior lawyers who become skilled editors can pass those skills on to their supervisees.

In fact, editing is only one of the supervisory skills that senior lawyers must possess. One of the complaints most frequently heard from young lawyers these days is that they don't receive enough feedback and supervision. Few senior lawyers have ever taken the time to think systematically about their supervisory skills. Even fewer have been exposed to workshops on supervisory skills that could help them deliver negative as well as positive feedback.

We're still learning about in-house training. The next challenge will come in imparting important but elusive skills: applied ethics, sound business practices, and common sense. Even these, however, can be confronted in training workshops. We are discovering that carefully conceived hypothetical cases are as useful in these areas as in conventional programs teaching skills like trial practice and negotiation. A lawyer must balance ethics, sound business practice, and common sense, for example, when deciding how much time to invest in a relatively small matter.

There are important reasons for planning and implementing professional development programs that transcend the practical. A good program may investigate professional responsibility. It can be a way to help restore the collegiality between older and younger lawyers, and improve communication among a firm's various departments. It can provide opportunities to discuss professional goals beyond the ad hoc imperatives of the firm's current case load. It can foster a sense of law as part of the humanities. Some lawyers would like to see in-house programs that develop major law firms into something like medical centers, combining practice, research, and education.

Although there have been and will be changes, the problem of professional development has concerned lawyers for a long time. In 1769, John Adams worried about adding a second young lawyer to his office: "What shall I do with two Clerks at a Time? And what will the Bar, and the World say? For their Advancement I can do little, for their Education, much, if I am not wanting to myself and them."

How to Get Your Training Program Started

In the chaotic field of in-house training, experience is perhaps the most significant factor in a program's success. There is no accepted wisdom, but over the past few years we have devoted considerable time and attention to some specific problems. Over the past six years we have accumulated a fair amount of experience. We help law firms plan training programs, provide in-house lawyering skills workshops, sponsor national lawyer training conferences, and cover lawyer training for *Lawyer Hiring and Training Report*, our monthly newsletter.

The practical sections of this book address vexing problems like managing and supervising lawyers, on-the-job training, burnout, and legal writing. We will discuss the myth of the mentor system, tactics for persuading skeptical partners that training workshops are not frivolous, the dusty disregard of most videocassette programs, the best ways to leverage your training investment, the appropriate mix between programs for business lawyers and those for litigators, the costs and benefits of hiring staff to manage your training efforts, and the differences between what associates want and what partners *think* associates want.

Above all, my advice is intended to be specific and practical. We will tell you what works and what doesn't, what's worth your time and money and what's not, when the conventional wisdom is sound, and when it is merely conventional.

Perhaps the question we're asked most often is: how do we get an in-house lawyer training program off the ground? The answer — it won't be easy — is often unwelcome. No new undertaking easily gains the approval of law firm management. And this one is tougher than most because not just money but — even worse — time must be committed. Add lawyers' resistance to the idea that formal training programs can improve lawyer performance, and you can understand why launching your training program may prove tougher than launching the U.S. space program. Remember, though, we did eventually get to the moon.

To begin, you need support from top management, whether it be the managing partner, general counsel, management committee, a venerable secretary or a radiant paralegal who quietly manipulates the whole organization. Even given a budget, you will fail without support from the top. Because unless your partners can be made to understand that their own rewards are in part linked to the success of the training program, they will kill it. Death may be sudden, through the kidnapping of associates signed up for the programs, or it may be slow and painful, through the relentless scorn and skepticism heaped on those who support your efforts.

However, firm management is likely to be more responsive to your proposed training program today than it might have been five years ago. First, other firms are doing it. You can use the old Macy's and Gimbel's routine. Second, many of your best hiring prospects want to join a firm with an effective training program. Realizing that their careers are more than ever likely to involve some moving around, they want to know what you will give them in return for what they do for you. Third, even skeptics among your partners are probably complaining about the lack of practical skills in new hires, and the lack of time senior lawyers have to impart those skills in old-fashioned ways. Fourth, many firms have grown so fast that young lawyers are now supervised by lawyers only a little older than themselves. These junior partners and senior associates are often enormously busy and obsessed with their own advancement in the firm. As a result, they may be less than perfect supervisors and mentors.

When you have lobbied the necessary support, you can begin to organize your training program. You need (much as I hate to say it) a committee. Call it something like the training committee or the lawyer development committee. Don't call it the CLE committee or your partners will think it exists only to approve registration for external CLE seminars. Don't call it the associate training committee; ultimately you will be offering programs for partners. (Henning & Associates' most popular training workshop focuses on supervisory skills for senior lawyers.)

The committee will want to find out what's going on in the lawyer training field. *Lawyer Hiring & Training Report*, the

Manual of In-House-Training, and LawLetters's conferences on lawyer training all can reduce the time and trouble you must invest in your basic education. Outside consultants can help you avoid the mistakes that others have made. (Why shouldn't you make your own distinctive mistakes?)

But there is no pill or magic potion to avoid the serious responsibilities of your undertaking. You can compare responsibility for your firm's training program to managing a major relocation, or a merger, or computerization. Only it's worse. Whereas those other management responsibilities eventually come to an end, the training committee should last as long as the firm itself. But you needn't grow old as its sole sustaining member.

After you know something about the field of lawyer in-house training, the committee will want to survey your firm's priorities. A word of caution: don't start with an elaborate trial skills program just because it's the most obvious and common. Perhaps that's where you should start, but it may be that 50 to 80 percent of your lawyers will never appear in any court except as a traffic law violator or party to a divorce. Think about it: how many of your trial lawyers will ever try a complex law suit? Most of them are (or should be) litigators, not trial lawyers. And litigators mainly budget cases and negotiate settlements before trial. Your corporate lawyers, too, are often negotiators. If you really want to get the most bang out of your training buck, perhaps your first workshop should involve negotiation or deposition-taking.

Whatever program you decide to try first, make sure your firm really needs it and can afford it. Don't spend the money on elaborate in-house programs to satisfy narrow, one-time needs. Don't seduce one of your partners into spending two weeks developing the definitive program on workouts, for example, if you plan to assign only one or two associates to such matters and PLI or ALI-ABA offers a better program.

Ideally, your own firm should supply all the faculty you need for a good in-house program. That ideal, however, is rarely attained because your colleagues are busy and may lack the interest or skills to become instructors. But keep the ideal in mind by bringing in outside instructors who not only can teach associates but who are also committed to proselytizing and training your partners in the best instructional techniques.

Don't assume that any clinical instructor at your neighborhood law school will succeed at teaching lawyers in your firm. Five years ago we used mostly law school clinicians in our programs. And we still use some because the best of them are very good indeed. But the best of them tend to be lawyers who teach part-time or move between careers in practice and the academy, rather than full-time law school professors. Your lawyers are busy, impatient, intolerant of jargon, resistant to **57** pointless touchy-feely games, and skeptical of training workshops in the first place. Put the wrong outsider in front of them, and you will set back your in-house training plans a decade if not a generation.

And finally, be modest. Remember James Joyce's line: "Leg over leg the poodle dog went to Dublin." Don't oversell in-house training to your partners. The fact is that training programs are successful if they achieve incremental gains in competence and productivity. They won't correct your hiring mistakes, or substitute for on-the-job experience, carefully supervised by senior lawyers willing to invest the necessary time and energy in their supervisory roles.

However, don't underestimate the value of formal training programs. You may spend between $5,000 and $75,000 to hire each new lawyer, and another $150,000 before that new lawyer begins to earn you any real profit. Modern practice thus demands that lawyers become capable and responsible as quickly as possible. If your training program speeds up the process by 10 or 20 percent, your bottom line — and your client's satisfaction — will improve considerably.

How Much Should
Lawyer Training Cost?

How much should a good in-house training program cost? Meaningful figures will include not only cash outlay but also the far stiffer cost of lost billing opportunities, or imputed costs. The cost is uncertain because the legal profession lags behind several others in developing training programs and thus not much hard data is available.

Some firms with formal training programs, including the far flung Baker & McKenzie and the 65-lawyer Boothe, Prichard & Dudley of McLean, Virginia, know they spend a considerable amount on training but have no means to track their expenditures. But we can piece together some useful benchmarks from the experience of pioneering firms and legal departments, comparable programs in other professions, and some commonly understood cash costs.

In 1982, Shearman & Sterling hired a full-time academic "dean," Donald C. Freeman (now with Baker & McKenzie), and developed a CLE budget that "approximates that of a small college," according to Freeman. How much does such a college spend per year? When asked, Freeman understandably became coy. But let's assume a small college has a student-faculty ratio of 12-to-one and pays its faculty an average salary of $30,000. If the college has 700 to 800 students, the faculty salaries alone amount to $1,800,000. That figure does not include overhead or any other expenses. Therefore, we can assume that Shearman & Sterling was spending $2 million or more in disbursements and imputed time for in-house as well as external CLE programs.

I imagine smoke beginning to emanate from the ears of senior lawyers reading these figures. Before they suffer permanent damage, let me quickly cool them out.

Even a top-of-the-line training program like Shearman &
Sterling's is relatively inexpensive. As of December, 1983, the
firm had 107 partners and 280 associates, or a total of 387
lawyers. Assuming that the firm devoted $2 million per year to
training lawyers, the budget per associate was little more than
$7,000. Any law firm competing for top law students knows that
it costs $5,000-75,000 per successful full-time hire. Most firms that
look carefully at their accounts also know that each new lawyer
costs another $100,000-$150,000 in billable hours written off,
wheel-spinning, salary, and overhead, before he or she truly
returns a profit to the enterprise. And, on the likely theory that
training programs benefit partners in one way or another as
much as associates, the average per lawyer cost of the Shearman & Sterling CLE program is only $5,000.

Thus — even at Shearman & Sterling — it costs far less to train
a lawyer annually than to finance the standard array of fringe
benefits. And training benefits the firm as much as it does the
individual lawyer. If, for example, a good writing program not
only improves the quality of legal writing but also increases a
lawyer's writing and editing efficiency by only 10 percent, the
firm will reap returns many times the cost of its training investment.

It's not just megafirms that have a serious investment in
training. James P. Hargarten, a partner in San Francisco's Thelen, Marrin, Johnson & Bridges, is a pioneer in developing
in-house training programs. Although he intentionally avoids
bookkeeping that would precisely tally the imputed costs of his
program, Thelen, Marrin's combined cash and imputed time
costs are apparently consistent with those of the much larger
Shearman & Sterling.

Hargarten estimates that his 100-lawyer San Francisco office
spends only $500 in cash for each of its approximately 55 asso-
ciates. This includes the occasional importation of outside instructors like those who helped Hargarten set up a deposition
training program. But each associate probably devotes 50 to 200
hours to training each year (the high end represents participation in comprehensive, clinical-style trial advocacy workshops).
And Hargarten's San Francisco partners devote considerable
time as instructors to both outside workshops and the in-house
program. Thus — at least in its litigation department — Thelen,
Marrin may be investing $7,500 or more per lawyer in cash and
imputed costs.

Even smaller firms that want to grow are beginning to budget
for training programs. Chicago's Much, Shelist, Freed, Denen-
berg, Ament & Eiger has grown rapidly to its present size of over
25 lawyers. To help maintain quality and compete with larger
firms for top-quality graduates, they are now offering training to

partners in supervisory skills and to associates in various lawyering skills — including negotiating and writing. Cash disbursements in the program's first year amounted to an average of about $400 per lawyer (partners and associates). Because associates will spend at least 20 hours participating in workshops, the firm invested approximately $2,000 per associate in the inaugural year of formal training programs.

But how does *your* firm decide what to invest? Major accounting firms budget approximately two percent of gross billings for training. But because accountants are often hired directly out of college, while lawyers must complete three years of postgraduate education, beginning lawyers have received more specialized training. Say what you will about law schools, they are better than no graduate training.

Also, accountants must follow specified routines that change periodically. Employers must insure that everyone is equipped to follow currently accepted accounting practices. Furthermore, the American Institute of Certified Public Accountants suggests that state certifying boards require 120 hours of continuing education over three years — or an average of 40 hours of accredited study per year — to maintain a certificate. (Significantly, the big firms have decided it is cost-effective to meet those mandatory requirements with extensive in-house training operations. If anybody should know what's cost-effective, it's the big accounting firms, I suppose.) So, two percent of gross billings is probably more than law firms need to invest in training.

To maintain standing in a speciality college, the typical annual continuing medical education requirement ranges from 35 to 50 hours per year. Perhaps new drugs and advances in surgical and medical techniques compel more rapid and frequent changes in medical practice than new developments in law and commerce do in legal practice. But is the medical profession, in quantitative terms, so much more "learned" than the law?

So what do you budget for training on a per lawyer basis? A firm needs to budget its time as well as money. As for time, mandatory CLE rules (in those misguided states that have adopted them) require 15 hours per year or less. A major criticism of mandatory rules is that 15 hours is merely cosmetic. One good writing workshop or trial skills program will take more than 15 hours.

I think a good lawyer, associates and partners alike, should devote a minimum of 25 to 30 hours per year to learning or teaching. This means that he or she can participate in a couple of clinical-style workshops, or attend semimonthly meetings of a specialty department, or travel to three CLE programs — hardly an onerous burden on practicing professionals. And these guidelines are really quite modest compared to the reality in some organizations. For example, one large East Coast firm that records the time its lawyers spend in training programs says recorded time ranges from 30 to 135 hours. Moreover, firm management believes that not all training time is being recorded.

Your cash costs will vary enormously, depending on the decisions you make. If you hire staff or assign paralegals to help administer the program, your cash costs will increase. If you hire outside consultants or instructors, you will pay them anywhere from $300 to $3,000 per day, depending on their ability and experience. But not hiring professionals may be even more costly in lost billable time. I am often amused to hear partners in large firms boast of their "cost-free" training program, fully administered and taught by themselves. In order to carry out routine administrative tasks for which they might have paid people at the rate of $10 to $100 per hour, they are sacrificing billable hours worth $150 to $300.

Partner time can often be profitably invested in lectures because they can reach an unlimited audience (including clients) and even be videotaped for repeat showings. However, most instructional efforts are too personalized to be warmed over and used again on videotape. And of course clinical-style workshops demand low student-faculty ratios.

Of course, partners and senior associates should keep as many instructional responsibilities for themselves as possible. But soon law firms will come upon two insights: First, many *administrative* chores in the training field can be delegated to the counterparts of recruitment coordinators. These training coordinators will not only be as competent as lawyers at a fraction of the cost but will do the job better. Second, teaching takes lots of time, as well as inclination and skill. In-house lawyers may be best at teaching substantive subjects and orienting new lawyers to the firm's traditions and idiosyncrasies. However, professionals may be better (as well as cheaper) at teaching other subjects, particularly those requiring practical skills. You will pay top dollar for any teaching or administering that your own lawyers carry out, so make sure you get your money's worth.

Twenty-five years ago hardly a firm would have said in-house training meant more than CLE, on-the-job supervision, and informal mentoring. None would have imagined that training could become a sizeable item in the budget. (Few firms had budgets.) But the same could have been said about management consulting, computerization, headhunting, public relations, and recruitment coordination. For better or worse, we practice today in a world where our costs go beyond rent, typewriter ribbons, and paperclips. Is it a better world? Who knows?

Good Training Programs Increase Profits

Many law firms operate under two hypotheses, one of which is right and the other dead wrong.

The first is that law firms make money on associates. Unless your firm is terminally inefficient and disorganized, you probably do profit from associates. To test this hypothesis, first look at associates' gross hourly billings and then deduct the uncollectable portion, as well as their salaries and fringes, overhead, and support expenses, including office space and secretarial. What's left is profit. In a well-managed firm, the profit on associates' work should amount to no less than 25 percent of your net profit, and may represent well over half.

The second hypothesis is that the cost of systematic lawyer training programs reduces a firm's profit. Nonsense. A good lawyer training program will actually increase the profit from associates. But however obvious this conclusion may seem to you and me, no doubt you confront partners who think training a waste of money, even if they don't say so. To help you persuade them, here are a few obvious ways in which training helps to improve the bottom line.

First training helps recruitment. You can't make money off associates you don't have. Yet firms find themselves competing as actively as ever for the best young lawyers because top-quality law graduates who can do the job at top-quality law firms remain scarce.

In fact, many firms that don't want to compromise their hiring standards discover that they can't fill their quota of new lawyers. For a busy firm, the economic result is disastrous. Let's **63** assume your young associates bill 2,000 hours per year at $75. If you fall short of your quota by four associates, you loose $600,000 of gross revenues from your income statement. If you are billing associates at $100 per hour and fall five short, you lose $1 million. Your own firm may bill fewer associate hours or charge a lower rate, but the point is the same.

Why does one recruiting program obtain its quota and another fail? Although there are lots of reasons, some relate to the training your firm is perceived to offer. Today, students choose law firms where they believe they will be well trained. Placement officers at the top 10 law schools will confirm that a reputation for excellent training counts for more than any other determining factor (except geography, which you can't do anything about).

Second, good training minimizes turnover. We estimate that a first-year associate costs a firm no less than $110,000 and possibly as much as $200,000, depending on recruiting costs. Factoring in lawyers' time and out-of-pocket charges, recruiting costs can range from $5,000 to $75,000. That's how much a firm will pay to recruit one full-time, entry-level associate. At these prices, associates who leave your firm after two or three years do not yield much profit. Unless they stay around long enough to amortize recruiting costs they will drain rather than enhance your resources.

Mid-level associates who leave their firms by choice most often say that they were not given a sense of career development or useful feedback concerning their work. Young lawyers want to know not only what you expect of them but whether or not they have fulfilled your expectations. And the backbone of a good lawyer training program is that it supplies such information.

Third, lawyer training can improve productivity. Let's use conservative figures to illustrate this point. Assume that your average associate represents gross collectable billings of only $112,500, which means that he or she is billing 1,500 hours a year at $75.

No training program is going to double a lawyer's productivity. Modestly assume that you can eke out a five percent productivity gain. Even given that minimal increase, your average associate will yield an additional $5,625. To determine your net profit, consider that the average per-lawyer cost of a good training program can be as little as $1,500 out of pocket. Then, if you assume that your average associate annually devotes a full week (40 billable hours) to training, the lost opportunity cost at $75 per hour is $3,000. Thus the total cost of training that associate is $4,500, and the net return at a five percent productivity gain is over $1,000. Now, if you can achieve productivity increases of 10 or 15 percent at little or no increase in the cost of training, think of what happens to your bottom line.

Finally, good training reduces law firm inefficiency. The key to efficiently providing legal services is for senior lawyers to delegate work to the lowest staff level at which it can be done well under good supervision. Yet which of you has not stayed late to rewrite hopelessly inadequate drafts from associates? Every time a senior lawyer does that, he or she costs the firm money in the short and long run. In the short run, I'll bet that few firms can bill out the extra work of the senior partner who is essentially duplicating the work done inadequately by the associate. Any firm that tried to do so would eventually discover that other firms with training programs that worked could boast of more competitive billing rates. And in the long run, the associate is not getting the editing and feedback that will make it possible for him or her to do it right next time. So the pattern repeats itself.

The absence of good training results in costly inefficiency. Many senior lawyers follow the path of least resistance when they assign work: they tend to give work to the associates who have done it before. If Sally is good at answering written interrogatories, Sally may find herself doing it over and over for years. If Charlie knows how to prepare the closing documents for real estate syndications, Charlie will be called upon every time.

On an assembly line, these work allocations would be rational and expected. But Sally and Charlie were hired with the expectation that they might become senior lawyers — partners. And because every year they make more money, in the course of time you will be paying far too much for the work they're doing. That's inefficient in itself but they may also become frustrated and leave for a firm where their careers can develop faster. You pigeonholed them because they performed their jobs well, and now you've lost them. If they don't choose to leave on their own, you may fire them because they apparently have stagnated, failed to fully develop their professional skills. Indeed that is exactly what happens. And it's your fault.

These inefficiencies are compounded when the pattern is repeated because, while your older associates were pigeonholed, you were hiring new lawyers and retarding their development, too. The younger associates were not trained to do the jobs "cornered" by Sally and Charlie. Inefficiency was piled atop inefficiency, with costly implications for your bottom line.

And yet, good training goes well beyond the bottom line. Notice — I have not once mentioned that training is likely to improve the quality of your firm's legal services. Nor did I even hint that you have a professional responsibility to provide good training to the next generation of lawyers. Nor does anything I've said indicate that training raises morale, keeps the blood flowing in the brains of old and young alike, and may even be fun.

Instead, I attempted to focus on the economics of lawyer training. The bottom line? The bottom line is that associates should make you money, and training them right should make you even more.

Once You've Recruited Your New Lawyers, You Must Recruit Them Again

Every year, you must recover from the recruiting season. It was agony to get the new lawyers you want and need. Guess what? As soon as they start work the following fall, it will be time to start recruiting all over again. I'm not talking about your next entering class. I'm talking about recruiting the same lawyers you just hired.

You struggled to get these recruits, pouring endless hours and extravagant sums into campus interviewing, flybacks, the summer clerk program, every possible technique. Our studies indicate that most firms spend between $5,000 and $75,000 to recruit each full-time lawyer. It takes years to amortize those costs, along with their salaries and other overhead. On any realistic accounting basis, you don't begin to make money on associates for two to three years.

Then, just when these associates are likely to become profitable, they become most desirable to predators. Yes, there are lots of opportunities out there for the best of your young lawyers. Headhunters lurk behind every bush, waiting to lure them off. You don't want to lose them, certainly not before they have justified your very substantial investment in them.

But what do you do to keep the ones you want? First, try to understand why the ones you lost decided to leave. Unfortunately, your own exit polls are likely to be inaccurate. Departing associates frequently prevaricate, in some cases to avoid offense and in others to be as obnoxious and vengeful as possible.

We have undertaken exit polls for several firms. And our data may be more reliable than yours because we are neither responsible for associates' unhappiness nor in a position to impair their careers. What follow are the reasons the best and the brightest young lawyers most often cite for departing from firms that wished them to stay.

Although young lawyers often complain about the quantity of work they are burdened with, few decide to leave a firm merely because of hours. "Too much work" is often a euphemism for not enough challenging work. Mary may be a whiz at preparing the closing documents for real estate syndications. But Mary will not stick around forever while her peers and younger lawyers are moving into more responsible work. She has become the permanent vassal of one or two real estate lawyers who don't want to invest the training time necessary to replace Mary with younger lawyers and move her up the ladder.

Freddy the fourth-year associate never gets into court because he must compete with junior partners as desperate as he for courtroom experience. But if the senior lawyers unnecessarily insist on taking courtroom appearances for themselves, Freddy and your other litigation associates are likely to get pretty frustrated.

In addition, inexperienced lawyers are too often given a job to do with little background on the client or the matter, and no guidance as to what needs to be done. Although they are told, "My door is always open if you need help," they find it practically impossible to break into their supervisors' schedules to get any meaningful assistance. Although most firms try to make forms, checklists, and other precedents available, too often these are inaccessible to inexperienced lawyers.

The lack of feedback is also a problem. Most firms think adequate feedback is provided for in the annual or semiannual performance review. Nonsense — there's less to those reviews than meets the eye. How does it benefit an associate's development to know that an anonymous partner didn't like a particular research job five and a half months ago? How useful is it for an associate to be told generally that he needs to work on his writing, when nobody has bothered to sit down and go over manuscripts with him?

The fundamental problem is that associates too often hear nothing at all from those who assigned them the work. In many cases they never even see the finished product. They don't know whether their effort was worthwhile or the senior lawyer had to start over from scratch. Useful feedback must come within days of the job being critiqued. It must be specific and include suggestions for improvement. At a minimum, young lawyers should always get a copy of any revised work. But too often they don't. And although feedback must sometimes be positive, too often new lawyers hear from the boss only when they have screwed up.

Law firm traditions of secrecy inhibit other kinds of communications. In the olden days, it was okay to construct an iron curtain between associates and partners. Law firms could hide all information about the firm's management, finances, and business development. And the consequences of such secrecy were minimal. Although life wasn't easy for a new lawyer in those days, it was relatively simple. The outcome of his employment was predictable: If he (there were virtually no shes) didn't make partner, the firm was usually able to place him as general counsel with one of the many corporations it served. If he did make it, that was soon enough to be brought by the priests into the sanctum sanctorum, to be anointed and have the dark secrets of the brotherhood disclosed.

But things have changed. The fortunes of law firms ebb and flow faster than those of New York discos. Not only on Wall Street, but on Main Street new lawyers can't be certain they will make partner. Indeed, who can predict whether the firms they join will even exist in seven years? Or if they're lucky and the chosen firms survive, they may change radically. A friendly, laid-back firm of 25 lawyers might become the Albuquerque office of Finley, Kumble or Skadden, Arps. Or a small family law partnership might merge with a local giant. Large or small, the firm could decide to limit offers of equity ownership and offer only permanent salaried employment. One or more senior practitioners in the new lawyer's chosen department might bolt for a different firm. If that happens, the new lawyer might or might not be invited to come along.

Today, major clients are likely to take huge portions of a law firm's business elsewhere or to disappear through merger or acquisition — friendly or unfriendly. Within the firm, new offices may be opened and as quickly spun off or shut down. As a result of such flux, the firm's need for lawyers may quickly increase or decrease.

With such a multitude of risks at hand, no wonder that your most talented associates fear the worst if you keep them in the dark. These aren't the olden days. Furthermore, management studies suggest that when employees don't know the truth, they imagine things to be worse than they are. So associates without knowledge are likely to be associates with troubling insecurities about their future in your firm.

The lack of formal training programs also creates problems. Young lawyers want two kinds of training. First, they want to learn the diverse skills necessary to succeed in your firm. If you pigeonhole them, like poor Mary in the example above, they will read the handwriting on the wall and get out fast. Second, because they know that the uncertainties of the legal world make it less probable every year that they will be offered partnerships in your firm, they also want training for lives in the law

elsewhere. If they sense that they are being trained in an esoteric and narrow specialty, useful only to you and your clients,
they may decide to bolt at the first opportunity.

Formal training programs can offer young lawyers depth,
sharpening their skills and focusing on the subtleties of the fields
they concentrate in. But they can also offer breadth, presenting
seminars in related areas and even encouraging crossover
learning between transactional and litigation lawyers.

Perhaps these problems seem insurmountable, based as they
are on underlying restlessness in the legal world today. Still, the
well-managed firm should be able to avoid losing hard-earned
and costly recruits. The answer in large part is to establish a
solid, systematic training program. Two of the fundamental
objectives of training are, first to lure better recruits in the first
place and, second, to keep the best.

Another way to express these objectives is, "First you have to
recruit, and then you have to recruit the same people all over
again." A good training program will resolve the issues raised
by disaffected young lawyers: work assignments, supervision,
feedback, intraoffice communications, and the need for broadly
based skills.

With a good training program, will you retain all of the
lawyers you wish to retain? Obviously not. But the costs of
turnover, inefficiency, and poor morale are enormous. If you
can retain some of those who might otherwise go and keep the
rest happy and committed, training costs will pale in compari-
son with these benefits.

And you need not sacrifice your clients' interests or your
personal income in an effort to transform your law firm into a
graduate school. Young lawyers want to know that you care
and that you are doing what you can to help them develop.
They know that you can't do everything.

You don't expect a new lawyer to be as accomplished as
yourself. Nor do new lawyers expect your firm immediately to
offer the ideal training program. They know your first efforts
may not be totally successful. They look for the same things in
you that you look for in them — commitment and gradual improvement.

Developing an
In-House Program

Creating an In-House Lawyer Training Program: Some Guidelines

There is nothing new about training lawyers within the firms, corporate legal departments, and government agencies where they practice. Before law school degrees were required for admission to the bar, the training was called "reading law" or "clerking." Some pretty good lawyers — John Adams and Abraham Lincoln, for example — received all their legal training that way. Article clerkships are still required in many common law jurisdictions. After law degrees became a prerequisite for practice, new lawyers continued to be trained on-the-job in those skills that law schools didn't teach.

Today, however, many firms are abandoning the old methods of training. Why? For the same reasons that led them to abandon old methods of running their offices. The brave new world of efficient law office management and sophisticated office machinery has rendered traditional methods obsolete. Similarly, rapid growth, higher costs (especially the cost of associates), increasingly complex legal matters, and client pressure to keep fees down have affected lawyer training along with other aspects of legal practice.

The benefits of developing a good program are substantial. Don't, however, ignore the costs. Some cash expenditures are inevitable, but the biggest cost will be your lawyers' time in planning, teaching, and learning. Moreover, merely understanding the need for and the costs of in-house training does not guarantee an effective program. Computerization offers an analogy: many law firms recognized the need to computerize their operations, yet we have all heard pathetic stories about the consequences of poor planning and implementation of computer installations. Poor planning for in-house training can also be painful — and costly. What follows is a set of guidelines that we have developed through experience with lots of law firms.

1. *Don't rely on law school training.* The practice of law and the skills it requires change faster than law school curricula — even clinical curricula — can adapt. Cases and problems used in law school clinics and skills workshops are unlikely to resemble the actual practice that graduates will undertake with your firm. Furthermore, every firm is unique, and the best place to teach its own lawyers how to practice its own brand of law is right there.

2. *Take advantage of all opportunities for external training and CLE programs.* Every firm, even the largest, has limitations on the training programs it can develop. Shearman & Sterling, for example, has an elaborate program within its litigation department but also sends some senior associates to the National Institute for Trial Advocacy. That makes sense because no firm can mount an intensive program lasting over several weeks and conducted by national faculty. Also, external training programs and CLE seminars will almost invariably be more cost-effective. The challenge is to learn not only what is available but also which programs are worth attending.

You can pay a big price for ignorance. A busy partner at a large Boston firm, for example, spent weeks preparing an in-house seminar on securities law. Although excellent, the seminar was no better than several offered by external providers like the Practising Law Institute, ALI-ABA, the American Bar Association, and the Law Journal Seminars-Press. In fact, external programs would have been more useful to that firm's securities lawyers because they offered several different and creative perspectives. The firm was clearly a loser when the cost of the internal seminar was compared with the cost of an outside securities program.

3. *Emphasize skills training.* Law schools teach one skill extremely well: how to analyze legal cases. CLE providers offer information on substantive legal issues. For the most part, however, legal skills are not taught anywhere. These skills include interviewing and counseling clients, negotiating, and writing. Trial skills, of course, are also important. NITA provides high-quality training in this area. Litigation training modeled on NITA is provided within many firms. However, pretrial and negotiating skills are even more important: more lawyers take depositions and make settlements than try cases in court.

4. *Plan your program with care.* Many firms have wasted time and money by embarking on programs before they were ready. Take the time to frame your objectives and decide how to reach them. For example, if you are considering a program in

legal writing, you might ask the following questions: a) What writing problems do you want to tackle? b) What resources are available to your firm for teaching the program you wish to offer? c) Will you retain outside instructors or use lawyers from the firm? d) How will lawyers be selected for the program? e) Will the program be voluntary or compulsory? f) How much money per lawyer are you willing to spend? g) How much time per lawyer are you willing to spend? h) How will you decide whether the results justified the costs?

5. *Recognize that in-house training involves more than formal instructional programs.* Lawyers learn in a variety of ways. One firm hired a full-time lawyer to supervise the small cases handled by young litigators. Another firm surveyed its lawyers and learned that advance sheets would be more widely read if they were received at home. Now every lawyer in the firm may request home delivery of advance sheets. And most important, train your senior lawyers how to supervise and give feedback to juniors.

6. *Don't attempt to initiate a program without the strong support of senior management.* Training efforts take time and cost money. Without the absolute commitment of senior management, a training policy is pointless. The practice of law is an endless succession of emergencies, interruptions, and crises, and no training program can be insulated from every emergency. On the other hand, lawyers must understand that disruptions must be kept to a minimum. To achieve this objective, senior management needs to demonstrate its commitment by deeds. And we all know that the only meaningful deed is to consider each lawyer's support of the training program when money is distributed.

7. *Support also must be pervasive among the partners.* A successful training program demands the support of virtually the entire firm. Whether or not partners are involved as instructors, they ought to understand the nature of the program, its objectives, and its demands on associates. No associate can be expected to give adequate time and attention to a training program if his or her boss is signaling that training sessions have no importance compared to work assignments. One way to build support among partners is to have them participate in the program. Also, when it comes to skills training, seeing is believing, and the learning curve in skills workshops can be dramatic.

8. *Ask associates what they think they need.* We find that partners and associates can perceive training needs very differently. In one firm, for example, partners planned to add training in "office skills" (interviewing, counseling, negotiating, and legal writing) to their existing program in trial skills. But our interviewers discovered that associates in the litigation de-

partment were unhappy with the trial skills program. The firm revamped its approach to trial skills and created the additional programs as well. In another firm, associates griped about the number of partners who regularly participated in external CLE seminars but apparently had no time for their own associates. We recommended that partners repeat their outside presentations for interested colleagues within the firm.

9. *Ascertain your internal training resources.* Ideally a law firm will supply all the necessary instructors for its training programs. Outsiders can rarely serve its needs as well. That ideal, however, is rarely achieved. Baker & McKenzie brought on a full-time director of training who has in turn retained outside instructors for some programs, including legal writing and other office skills. Pitney, Hardin, Kipp & Szuch of Morristown, N.J. retains outside instructors for skills training while partners offer substantive seminars.

One barrier to supplying your own instructors is the value of your senior partners' time. You can assume that each three-hour workshop will require a minimum of nine hours' preparation. Nor is time the only deterrent: some lawyers are skilled practitioners but terrible teachers. And effective teaching requires an open and trusting relationship. Thus young lawyers may progress faster with outside instructors, trained in clinical teaching methods, who form no part of the hierarchy that decides on salaries and partnerships. (A random selection of law school instructors, however, will rarely serve a firm's training needs adequately).

10. *Take advantage of audiovisual resources.* The intelligent use of video equipment greatly enhances skills training. Lawyers, like other human beings, practice denial. They will not believe that they did or said something until they see it played back on videotape. In addition to mirroring faults, videotape is an excellent medium for demonstrating prowess.

Also, many publishers and CLE providers are now producing educational videotapes that can usefully supplement live training programs within the firm. Lawyers who might decline to prepare a seminar entirely on their own are often delighted to provide live commentary to a videotape presentation. And the interaction of videotape and live discussion can be stimulating and effective.

11. *Be modest in what you expect from a training program.* Nobody knows exactly how the best lawyers learn to practice. Obviously we learn in many ways, beginning in grammar school or even earlier. Lawyers will probably always learn most from practice itself. However, the high cost of everything today (including errors and omissions) means that even an incrementally successful training program is more than justified. For example, if a good writing program enables lawyers to write

and edit five percent faster and better than they could before, the costs of the program, amortized over their careers, are certainly justified. On the other hand, no one should expect a writing program to transform an average writer into Mark Twain or even Benjamin Cardozo.

12. *Use training to encourage vertical and horizontal cross-fertilization.* Often the best moments in a formal training program are the informal exchanges between associates and partners. Too often the pace of modern practice precludes all but the most hurried professional discourse between a firm's senior and junior lawyers. We find, however, that skills workshops often stimulate exchanges between partners and associates on billing, fees, conflicts of interest, and other important topics, during which partners can share with associates the firm's approaches to these issues.

Similarly, departmental lines should not artificially restrict participation in workshops focusing on skills important to all lawyers, such as negotiating and writing. As firms grow and become more departmentalized, not enough opportunities arise for specialists in separate departments to share work and ideas. But skills training workshops can be a useful forum for this purpose.

13. *Don't exclude partners from learning as well as teaching opportunities.* Writing and editing are good examples of skills in which partners often need help as much as associates. We have found that it does little good to help associates write with greater clarity, precision, and conciseness if their bosses compel them to rewrite in obscure, ponderous, verbose prose.

Sadly, our profession is much less learned than medicine: the best doctors combine practice, learning, and teaching throughout their careers. In-house training programs may be the legal profession's first step toward integrating these three activities.

Involve As Many People As You Can in Designing Your Training Program

Lawyer training within the firm is so new that it's like Dr. Johnson's description of the dog that walks on two legs: "It's not that he does it well, but that he does it at all." You may have a good seminar here and an exhilarating workshop there, but most law firms don't have a training program.

I mean that your training efforts are probably not directed at the problems that most seriously blunt your professional performance. Instead, you devote training resources to areas that interest you personally, or to those which other lawyers in the firm are willing to participate, or to which senior management directs you. Most in-house programs are the training equivalent of the journalistic maxim: "All the news that fits, we print."

To be sure, sometimes the best way to launch a lawyer training program is simply to launch it — do what you can when you can. But sooner or later your skeptical partners will question its arbitrary and occasional character. You'll arm your opponents with reasons for junking the program, and you'll diminish your support among the faint of heart. But, with a coherent design for your training program, you can plan, budget, assign priorities, and effectively defend it against natural predators.

The best way to design your program is to involve as many of your colleagues as possible. By doing so, you weaken the we-they syndrome. Those involved in the planning necessarily invest something of themselves in the project, and will likely feel that the final product responds to their needs.

Before you ask for their participation, however, decide on the program's fundamental framework. Will it be firm-wide, or entirely segregated by legal specialties? Will you include lawyers in satellite offices, or will you encourage them to plan their own programs? We find that the best approach combines firm-wide offerings with offerings for which each department or geographical location bears the major responsibility. Firms may vary, but usually it's easier to sell a program with a variety of activities designed to appeal to different units. If you do take this approach, you will want to involve representatives from each unit.

Your next step is to decide who gets training. Typically, firms zero in on entry-level associates. But as growing numbers of firms and corporate legal departments hire lawyers laterally, the training picture obviously changes.

Remember, too, that you will waste resources and possibly raise the anxiety level among young lawyers by offering workshops on subjects and skills that they will not use for years, if ever. It's not that corporate lawyers shouldn't know something about litigation and vice versa, but you should avoid teaching negotiating skills to new lawyers two or three years before they will ever need them. Whatever approach you choose, however, the lawyers involved as learners and teachers must somehow be convinced that they "own" the program design.

Next you must identify and recruit the people who will participate in the design of the curriculum. Consider three groups. The first is your curriculum committee. It could be the training committee. Or you might want to ask representatives of the training committee to sit with other key senior and mid-level lawyers as a curriculum subcommittee. I prefer the latter approach because you can factor in a broader range of thinking and — equally important — expand your support constituency. The curriculum committee should solicit recommendations for workshops and seminars, review them, and design a coherent curriculum.

Next the curriculum committee should identify a second group, the "subject matter specialists" — lawyers and others, inside and outside the firm, who know the subjects and skills to be taught and can construct the workshops and seminars. In asking these experts to work on the programs in their areas of expertise, try to get them to come up with more than a list of seminar topics and lecturers. Ask them first to identify what they think lawyers in their specialties should know or be able to do and then analyze how the current training program fails to do the job. Finally, they should draft a design for the new curriculum, including not only proposed subject matter and instructors but teaching methods (lecture, discussion, demonstration, simulation) and materials as well.

The third group to involve are the proposed students. Either integrate them into the curriculum committee or ask them to review the experts' draft before the curriculum committee finally acts upon it. Which alternative you choose may depend on the seniority of the students. If the program is designed for your entry-level lawyers, you may want to keep them off the curriculum committee, but let them look at the proposed curriculum before it goes into effect. Not only will they have some useful things to say, they will be far more enthusiastic about participating if they play a role in curriculum development.

Typically, lawyers responsible for training have not involved the maximum number of their colleagues in the curriculum design process. Their reasons are compelling. Nobody else is interested. Those who are interested don't have time. The curriculum designed by a committee — or worse, several committees — is lucky if it is no uglier than a camel. Or the training partner might say that he or she is willing to plan a program but not to play social director to a bunch of irresponsible prima donnas.

What can I say in response? Only that, because every lawyer considers himself or herself independent, law firms and even corporate legal departments are organizations only in the loosest sense. Still, your best solo efforts are less likely to be implemented than a minimal group effort. Better you should begin with a modest training program that has been designed and reviewed by as many lawyers as possible, than an epic program, your personal magnum opus, that will be respected but not used.

How to Prevent Videotape Machines from Gathering Dust in Law Offices

By now your firm very likely has purchased or is contemplating purchasing videotape equipment. A recent ABA survey sampled about 46 firms and legal departments interested in CLE and discovered that almost 83 percent owned videocassette playback machines and 72 percent owned video cameras.

Although there's lots of video hardware and software out there, much of it is not being used. Lawyers responsible for convincing their brethren to provide money for these gadgets are often disappointed because they are underutilized. These lawyers are confused about why video hasn't captivated and enlightened their colleagues, and they wonder what they can do about it.

Video has substantial potential in helping to train lawyers. But it has its limits. If you have purchased equipment — and consigned it to a musty storage closet — perhaps you will be stimulated to fetch it out and try again. If you haven't yet taken the video plunge, what follows may shape more realistic expectations than you might otherwise have generated.

Although video may turn out to be useful in other aspects of your practice — like recording testamentary executions, depositions, and even judicial testimony — let's assume that you are principally interested in using it to train lawyers. Effective training requires that you match learning objectives with teaching methods and tools.

Lawyers usually are interested in three different types of learning. The first, and most basic, involves the acquisition of cognitive information, which we traditionally get from books, lectures, advance sheets, and panel discussions. Second, in addition to black-letter information, lawyers must learn practical skills. Trying a law suit is an obvious lawyering skill, but others range from writing and editing to marketing legal services. We learn these skills through on-the-job training, demonstrations, and simulations. The third type of learning is the most elusive. This is the acquisition of common sense, good judgment, and even wisdom. The school of hard knocks is just about the only institution accredited to teach it, although on-the-job training and mentoring, with good feedback, can accelerate the speed at which we learn from our mistakes.

Video can transmit cognitive information to lawyers, but the cost in time and money is often high. And when it comes to teaching common sense and good judgment, video can do almost nothing. Video excels only in the second learning mode — the acquisition of practical skills.

The market in cognitive information is fairly well developed. Most CLE videotapes that you can purchase or rent offer cognitive information. At their worst, they show a bald-headed, glassy-eyed, nervous lawyer (often the chairman of a bar association section or committee) reading monotonously from a third-rate outline. At best, they offer a human dynamo, like Irving Younger, whose unforgettable style underscores fundamental points worth knowing.

The best and the worst, however, share certain limitations. In a given amount of time, neither can provide as much information on tape as we could absorb from the printed page. In fact, the bravado performance may convey less essential information than the hopelessly boring talking head. Nor are viewers before the boob tube able to participate by comment, question, or debate. Lawyers who advocate high-tech learning tools need to be reminded that the printed word was in its time a high-tech breakthrough, and still has its place. Many cognitive learning needs continue to be best served by the printed word.

"But," say you, "there are some things that I just can't get my associates to read." Harvard sociologist Daniel Bell sees your point: "We are living in an increasingly visual culture. People who originally got much of their information from speaking or reading are now getting their facts from TV and computer screens." Perhaps your youngest associates are the illiterate progeny of TV: perfect candidates for live CLE or videotapes. Tapes may even serve them better than live CLE because the tapes are carefully edited in contrast with the time wasted at live CLE programs. Creative editing, done by expert video producers like Michael D. Hofmayer of California CEB, can contribute significantly to a CLE program.

Furthermore, humans being what they are, some simply won't remember what they read in James Casner's *Estate Plan-*

ning — even if you can get them to pick it up. But they may never forget what the great man himself intones on the tube in National Practice Institute's ABA videotape, *The Use of the Revocable Trust in Estate Planning*. Sure, you could travel to Cambridge for the Harvard summer program for lawyers, but that costs infinitely more time and money than a videotape.

Some studies even suggest that videotape may be a better teaching technique than live performance. Research at the University of Iowa College of Law suggests that law students (and, by extrapolation, lawyers) generally retain more information taught via television than live lectures.

You can easily overcome the worst feature of canned CLE by adding your own ingredients before serving. In-house experts can present live commentary. They will want to prepare for these sessions, but much less than they would for a solo lecture. Or make your own in-house videos. If your in-house training program includes sessions presented by partners, video can both maximize their impact and minimize the time spent. Lectures can be taped and replayed for absentees. Some taped lectures have a long shelf life, awing new recruits for years to come.

Lawyers are not yet in the habit of reaching for a videotape as they might a book. You must inculcate that habit. Make your videotape equipment accessible. Put it on a cart so it can be wheeled into anybody's office. Make sure the equipment is easy to use, functional, and functioning. Get your best draftsmen to type out instructions so simple even a lawyer can understand them, and tape them to the side of the machine. Some firms have established regular schedules for video presentations, with or without live commentary. Pitney, Hardin, Kipp & Szuch, in Morristown, New Jersey, offers a lunchtime program and provides sandwiches and coffee to encourage attendance.

Still, video as a tool in teaching cognitive skills is somewhat controversial. But ask anybody who has used video to teach trial tactics, negotiation, client interviewing and counseling, or any other communications skills, and they will tell you that video is invaluable. The aphorism goes, "Tell me and I'll forget; show me and I'll remember; involve me and I'll understand." A simple, easily operated video camera, along with your videocassette recorder, will give you the opportunity to "show" through demonstrations and "involve" through taped simulations.

Demonstrations can be purchased from CLE producers, or you can tape your own. Either way, they afford associates the chance to see experienced lawyers in action, and to see them again and again. Even if you never buy a videotape of a lecture or panel discussion, you may want to consider purchasing tapes of demonstrations to help your associates more quickly learn how to handle themselves as practitioners.

But perhaps the most effective training program you can develop will be to tape your associates' performance in simulations of lawyering skills. It's easy to deny that you physically moved away from opposing counsel when you told him a "stretcher" during a simulated negotiation. But the videotape never lies! A young litigator may not be conscious of his leering, abusive style of cross-examination. It's one thing to be told about it and quite another — far more profound — to see himself doing it on tape.

The object of these simulations is not to ridicule or humiliate participants, but to offer feedback that can help them correct their faults and improve their technique. The learning curve on lawyering skills goes up steeply when supervisory feedback is supplemented with video recordings of lawyer performance. And, best of all, the mistakes made in videotaped simulations are cost-free to the client and to the firm's professional liability policy.

Moreover, videotape gives you the flexibility, with or without outside instructors, to critique lawyers' performances in training sessions with their peers present, or in private. The prevailing atmosphere in your office can determine the choice.

When it comes to common sense, good judgment, and wisdom, however, these things are not easily taught — and high-tech devices won't help. Professional judgment comes from carefully supervised on-the-job experience, supplemented by wise counseling. Neither is facilitated by video. But don't reject a useful tool because it can't solve all your problems.

There are a few other balloons associated with video that need to be pricked. The biggest one, filled mainly with hot air, is the "real time" video extravaganza. First offered by microwave relay, later by telephone hookup, and most recently by satellite, these link scores of sites to present "live" CLE seminars. Before signing up for one, ask what you will gain by witnessing a "live" video event. Occasionally, a legal development is so important to lawyers and clients that all of us need to know as much as we can about it as fast as we can. For most lawyers, the last time that happened was the Tax Reform Act of 1976. Before that, perhaps the Supreme Court slaughter of the National Recovery Act, and then we might have to go back to the *Dred Scott* decision.

Let's face it, for better or worse, the law changes slowly, and United Parcel Service can deliver a videotape soon enough for virtually all CLE purposes. Not only can we wait, but by waiting we may get a tighter, edited version of the live spectacle. Satellite teleconferencing, John Naisbitt predicts in *Megatrends*, "is another trend that will not happen."

Naisbitt also says that high-tech innovations lead to "high touch" counterattacks: "The more technology we introduce into society, the more people will aggregate, will want to be with other people." So don't expect much solo viewing of CLE video-tapes. Accommodate human resistance to the high-tech of video by organizing high-touch viewing situations with as much human interaction as possible.

Video can play a dazzling variety of roles in lawyer training. But it is not a magic solution. It cannot liberate your partners from responsibility for hands-on supervision and formal train-ing. Video will reach its potential as a valuable but limited tool when we stop arguing that it's everything, or nothing.

Should You Hire Staff for Your In-House Program?

Although only a handful of law firms have hired professional staff to administer their in-house training programs, many more have begun to consider the possibility. So here are a few suggestions to help guide you when your firm gets the urge.

Hiring training staff should be one of the last things you do, not the first. There are good reasons for hiring staff, but not when you're just starting out. Think of an in-house lawyer training program as a vehicle to get your firm from one place to another. Do you want a Subaru or a Jaguar? Do you need a sports car or a bus? Are you hiring an automotive engineer, a mechanic, a chauffeur, or a parking lot attendant?

Don't hire anybody until you can answer the equivalent questions about your in-house training program. Hiring professional staff only seems like a good starting place. Shearman & Sterling had a comprehensive lawyer training program for many years before it hired its first director of CLE. Paul, Hastings, Janofsky & Walker hired a training director as part of a firm-wide effort to become more management-oriented. Baker & McKenzie commissioned a thorough outside study of its training needs before it began searching for its first director of professional development. And the process of selecting their second director proved to require almost as much internal discussion and review as the initial undertaking.

Hiring staff to do the planning for you is a definite mistake. Whoever you hire will naturally steer toward a plan in which he or she fits. For example, you may primarily need training in communications skills — written and oral. But if you hire a

89

systems planner or a professional educator from one of our typical schools of business, or education, or social psychology, he or she is likely to be even less sensitive to language than the typical law school graduate. The jargon and circumlocution quotients in those fields are incredibly high. If, on the other hand, you hire an elegant stylist and editor to help you in the planning stage, you may fail to discover your firm's training needs for other legal knowledge and skills.

Furthermore, you should postpone your staff hiring because a good in-house training program requires solid support from virtually all of your partners, even from its inception. They must be prepared to participate. You won't have a very good program if your best lawyers are not sharing what they know. Whether or not they participate as instructors, they had better participate in planning and by encouraging or requiring younger lawyers to attend the program. If you have already attempted to mount some workshops or seminars, you know how devastating it can be when many participants do not show up because their bosses have sent signals that the program is less important than billable hours. Forget about a more comprehensive program for which you've hired staff if you have not developed an extremely high level of commitment from your partners. You can be sure that if your partners won't respond to the urging of firm management on training, they will be even less receptive to recommendations from hired help.

We all know, in the abstract, that it's folly to hire anybody without an adequate job description. Nevertheless, blind faith sometimes overcomes us and we expect a stranger brought into the bizarre and complex world of a law firm to be a *deus ex machina*. It simply won't work: an administrator can't do it all. You need to know through experience, not promises, how much effort your own lawyers are willing to expend in planning and teaching. You need to know through experience how much training your lawyers need and how much your firm can afford in time and money. The time that can be committed will almost always be less than the time you believe should be committed.

After your program is up and running, you will know whether you need an administrator to oversee the scheduling and collating of materials; a systems expert to get your precedents (forms and checklists) in shape and on line so that they can be effectively utilized; a teacher to conduct a fair portion of the classes; or a trainer to help your own lawyers become more effective teachers. In truth, all of these responsibilities usually require some attention. But you won't know the proper mix for your program until you have attempted it all yourself.

When you think you're ready to hire training staff, pause again. Even if you've been at it for years, chances are that controversy and dissent continue about your goals, methods, and (especially) expenditures for in-house training. The decision whether or not to hire staff may be weighted towards the power in your firm. If at this point you pause long enough to objectively appraise where you are and where you want to go, you can make a more rational decision. You could ask a fair-minded partner previously uninvolved in the program to conduct this appraisal for you. However, he might have to spend a lot of time learning what's been done and what's practical to do next. If so, consider importing a consultant who can devote undivided attention to the problem.

Consider a wide range of staffing possibilities:

1. *The recruitment administrator model.* In several firms, recruitment administrators have already demonstrated interest in training programs. They have undertaken studies of available resources and helped coordinate workshops. This is not a bad model. Lawyers must be intimately involved in the hiring process, but there are mountains of work for which they have neither the time nor the administrative talent. A comprehensive training program requires organization, research, and administration that recruitment administrators could provide.

Recruitment administrators tend to be bright, energetic, imaginative, and ultimately frustrated with their jobs. In the long run, then, most will be dissatisfied. But since hiring and training are two sides of the same lawyer development coin, it makes sense to assign administrative responsibility for both to the same office.

2. *The associate looking for an alternate career path.* At some point, legal training requires the involvement of lawyers. You may have in your midst right now an associate who is not obsessed with winning on the conventional partnership track but is highly regarded, understands your strengths and weaknesses, and would be an ideal director of lawyer development.

This approach raises some serious questions, though. Lawyers often have a hard time knowing how to relate to another lawyer in the firm who is neither a partner nor on the partnership track. Indeed, in this case, the lawyer would probably not be practicing law at all. This could be a fatal problem for some candidates in some firms, but an associate who has been around a few years ought to know whether he could endure the problems that this eccentric status might create.

3. *The lawyer cum trainer.* In rare cases, law firms have hired a lawyer for the dual roles of practitioner and trainer. The problem is that this job is inherently unstable. In every case I have observed, the lawyer eventually has opted for a conventional partnership (in the firm or elsewhere), or has sought a law school teaching job.

4. *The law school professor.* We tend to forget, but some law school professors have had practical experience; a few have **91**

even been partners. They may be prime candidates for some law firm training departments. But limit your search among law school professors to former practitioners because the more typical law school teacher marches to a different drummer than the in-house training instructor. Some professors are brilliant and scintillating every minute of their teaching careers. As a rule, though, law school professors can be as obscure, slow, and pedantic as they desire: the students are required to pay attention if they want to pass the course, and the distractions are relatively few and unimportant.

Furthermore, while professors have a semester or a full year to get their message across, you don't have that kind of time for in-house workshops or seminars. It's simply not necessary to devote that much time, but most law school professors can't make the adjustment. Only a handful of law school teachers have succeeded in our in-house training workshops. Most of them go up in smoke when confronted with busy lawyers, who quickly lose patience after a few minutes of useless abstractions and aimless intellectual meanderings.

5. *Educators.* There are two kinds of educators, those who have graduate degrees in a substantive field *and* know how to teach, and those who principally studied educational technique and methodology. With exceptions, the first category attracts people of broader and deeper intellect, who are likely to catch on to what a law firm does and to engage intellectually with your partners and associates. Educational methodology and technique are important, but they are quickly and easily acquired. Ten minutes is probably not enough time, but 10 hours may be more than adequate.

I spent a few years working intensively with educators as we developed a law-related education program for elementary and secondary schools. I also read a lot of material on teaching and education and concluded that the only important writing on educational theory was done almost a century ago by John Dewey. More recently, Jerome Bruner has had some interesting things to say, but they are in one or two essays easily consumed in an evening. I am not advising against hiring certified trainers or educators. But you should hire them on their merits as intelligent, capable people who happen to have such certificates. Don't be bewitched by the jargon.

Training is present-oriented, task-oriented, and repetitive. Lawyers need a lot of it. But they also need continuing *education*. Education tends to evolve and it involves ideas. Law is, after all, a learned profession, not merely a craft. You must decide whether the trainer you hire can also deal with education. Some can, and some can't.

The question often comes up as to how big a firm must be to justify a training staff. By now the answer should be pretty clear.

I know a firm of 25 lawyers in which one partner spends substantial time on lawyer training. If that firm had a coordinator, the partner in question would remain involved in some aspects of training because he likes it and he's good at it. But he could also practice more than enough law to pay for the new staff person.

Finally, there remains the question of compensation, which you'll need to address when considering whom to hire. Right now the salaries for training staff vary as widely as their backgrounds and job descriptions. The range is between $18,000 and more than $100,000. Whatever you end up paying, you will probably get your money's worth. The highest paid will make less than the partner who might otherwise do the same non-revenue-producing work. But don't pretend that your staff is responsible for the program's success. Only you and your partners can carry that load.

Training Women Lawyers:
There Is a Difference

Major law firms are hiring as many women law graduates as men — or more. No speakers disputed that fact at our conference, The Woman Lawyer Within the Firm: Expectation and Fulfillment. Nor could they dispute that women aren't advancing as fast or as far as their male peers.

The question is why. Some women obviously have interests that are incompatible with high-pressure corporate firm practice, and they prefer to pursue those other interests. But some who would like to make it don't. These women start off with academic credentials as good as or better than those of their male peers who do make it, so we must look further for answers.

If we were focusing on other disadvantaged sectors of American society, such as racial and cultural minorities, we would quickly look to see if they were getting less training, or poorer training than their majority counterparts. And possibly women lawyers do receive inferior training, even though no one is intentionally discriminating against them.

If women are unintentionally getting a raw deal, perhaps lawyer training can help to overcome their special problems. To explore this proposition, I want to look at lawyer training from several perspectives: Who is trained? Who does the training? How are the trainers trained? Should the training process recognize sexual differences? And finally, what subjects might we cover in lawyer training to help women lawyers progress more quickly in the firm?

Who gets trained? Lawyer training includes external CLE programs, the National Institute for Trial Advocacy and its **95** counterparts, formal in-house workshops and seminars, mentoring, and the day-to-day supervision of on-the-job work experiences. Women may get the short end in any or all of these training opportunities for at least two reasons.

First, some women simply spend fewer hours in the office than their male counterparts. These women lawyers may bill the same number of hours and produce work in every respect as good, but they do it more efficiently. In some cases, they find that law practice is enormously rewarding but so are their outside interests. They complete their work and don't hang around. Other women are formally granted maternity leave or work part-time. In either case, certain office-related activities have to be sacrificed. These may include formal training opportunities or informal supervision and mentoring sessions.

Some firms try to circumvent these problems by establishing a "full-time" policy for young associates. Brooksley Elizabeth Born, a partner and member of the management committee of Washington, D.C.'s Arnold & Porter, says that her firm is reluctant to offer part-time arrangements to women in the first three years of practice. Those are the critical training years, and training tends to be impaired if a lawyer — woman or man — gives the firm less than full time and attention during those years. After three years in which she gave the practice of law her undivided attention, Born took time off to have her first child and then worked part-time for several years.

Other firms have less well-defined policies. Roberta Ramo, managing partner of Albuquerque's Poole, Tinnin & Martin, recalls a brilliant woman lawyer at another firm who worked efficiently by keeping her door closed, discouraging informal conversation with other lawyers. She jogged at noon and left between five and six almost every evening. Naturally that woman had no time for CLE, in-house training, or informal talks with older lawyers who might have become her mentors. Until Ramo explained to her why she should stick around and stay in touch with other lawyers, that talented woman was destined to be yet another woman associate who inexplicably doesn't make it.

Second, most women today are supervised by men. Some of those men perceive that the firm's training investment in women is wasteful because — statistically — women are less likely to stay around and become profit centers. Almost every firm I visit includes partners who are anything but male chauvinist pigs but who nevertheless have serious misgivings about the recent large contingent of women recruits, mainly because women recruits have a higher turnover rate than male recruits. I needn't remind you that this is devastating to the bottom line. So it's not surprising that a recent study indicates that professional men are twice as likely as women to be given time off for training.

Typically, a supervisor decides whether a supervisee should go to a CLE workshop, or a NITA program, or the Harvard summer program for lawyers. Certainly, a supervisor will decide which young lawyers get the juiciest assignments and the most personal attention. If the supervisor believes the firm will never recoup the time and money invested in a particular woman, he may be reluctant to honor her requests for specific assignments or to initiate training proposals for her.

It is also important to consider who does the training. Traditionally, teachers have been important role models for their students. How many CLE faculty, in-house instructors or senior lawyers at this point are women? Relatively few, but some progress has been made. If you are not able to come up with senior women lawyers to be instructors, supervisors, and mentors, you might want to import one or more female instructors until your own ranks include senior women.

Here's an idea that might kill two birds with one stone. If you have women lawyers seeking part-time status after putting a lot of good experience under their belts, they might serve as in-house trainers or mentors. Frances Koncilja, a partner in the Denver firm of Horowitz & Koncilja, taught for NITA during her maternity leave. "It was a wonderful way to stay involved and then bring me up to speed once I got back into practice," she reported in NITA's newsletter. If your firm utilizes one or more of its part-time women lawyers as in-house instructors, they benefit both from the reduced pressures, and from a more predictable schedule. The firm benefits, too, because these women will remain closely involved with firm matters while they help solve your training problems, at least temporarily.

The computer revolution may solve some of the problems of women lawyers. Women compelled to be at home part of the work day will find that work can be done on computer terminals, connected by modem to the office computers. Through electronic mail, women at home will be less removed from their supervisors and mentors. (We may even discover electronic mail to be useful for feedback on assignments even when both parties are in the office.)

Studies in other professions indicate that women who fail to advance as quickly as their male counterparts are not receiving their fair share of challenging assignments. At The Woman Lawyer Within the Firm conference, several women confirmed that this is true in the legal profession as well. Studies have also documented that women do not get as much useful feedback, especially negative feedback, from their supervisors. In our experience, many male lawyer supervisors have admitted to difficulty in delivering negative feedback to women. So the trainers, mostly men, may not be prepared to train women.

Don't assume however, that male lawyers are terrific supervisors of male lawyers either. The fact is that most lawyers have never thought about what it takes to be a good supervisor of men or women lawyers, nor have many lawyers ever had any training in supervisory skills. One source of trouble is that supervisors delegating work, like other human beings, follow the path of least resistance. We give work to those we believe can do it most efficiently, a path not usually best for those who would like to learn how to do the job better.

It's also human nature to avoid criticizing others, men or women. Lawyers are even more reluctant than other professionals to offer constructive criticism, but too often better at demeaning young lawyers, particularly women. In the famous *Hishon* case involving Atlanta's King & Spaulding, almost no fact was in dispute except whether Elizabeth Hishon was given negative or positive feedback about her partnership prospects during her sixth year of practice with the firm. Strong legal reasons for clarity aside, ambiguity of this sort is not good for the associate or the firm.

Lawyers can be trained to be better delegators and assigners of work, better supervisors, and better sources of negative and positive feedback. If you are dissatisfied with the rate at which your women associates are moving through the firm, you might want to focus on training (or at least raising the consciousness of) your partners, rather than training associates exclusively.

Generalizations are never fully accurate, and in the area of sex discrimination, they can lead to dreadful and unproductive squabbles. So, recognizing that there are classic exceptions, I will nevertheless suggest that women generally begin their legal careers with somewhat different strengths and weaknesses than their male counterparts. Time after time, in law firms throughout the country, we have observed that women tend to start out as more skillful client interviewers and counselors, while men tend to start out as better negotiators.

Several panelists at The Woman Lawyer Within the Firm speculated that girls' friendships put a premium on being empathic, good listeners, and trusted counselors. Boys, on the other hand, often have fewer such friendships, but they are more likely to be involved in activities that depend on "win-win" negotiating techniques. Judith Richards Hope of the Washington, D.C. office of Paul, Hastings, Janofsky & Walker, and Sarah Moss of New York's Davis Polk & Wardwell, both speculated that women may be more zealous partisans on behalf of their clients in an effort to be more macho than men. Relentless advocates typically do not make great negotiators.

Many people resist the notion of gender differences, whether biological or sociological. However, if you visit a nursery school in an enlightened, liberal community, you can observe these differences, along with many similarities, in boys and girls at play. Recent data from the medical profession support my observations. Women doctors spend an average of 17 minutes with each patient, according to the National Center for Health Statistics. That's about four minutes more than the average for male doctors. Also, women doctors do more counseling of patients, according to Health Economics Research, a Boston think tank.

Thus, as a member of that think tank told the *Wall Street Journal*, "Women may provide higher quality care than men." Others suggest that women doctors may have fewer patients and consequently more time on their hands. But based on our observations of women lawyers, we believe that women are "naturally" better interviewers and counselors.

These natural talents can be used to a firm's advantage. Women, I believe, can teach their male peers how to be better interviewers and counselors, how to listen better, how to elicit all the information necessary from clients and how to develop more empathic client relationships. Similarly, men can teach women about the "game" of negotiating: how to keep personality out of it, how to help the other side understand its real interests, how to reach a compromise satisfactory to all parties. Whether or not I am right about the different skills of men and women, I am sure that your training programs will be the better for being designed with sensitivity to gender issues.

Finally, should there be different subject matter for training women? Many panelists at The Woman Lawyer Within the Firm said that subtle sexual harassment remains a problem in the legal profession. What's obviously discrimination to a woman lawyer may be unobservable to her male colleagues, especially the older ones. Why not offer workshops in sexual issues where men and women lawyers can discuss sex discrimination, sex stereotypes, sexual harassment, and the like? One of the panelists, N.Y.U. law professor Eleanor M. Fox, formerly a partner at New York's Simpson Thacher & Bartlett, published a novel, *W.L., Esq.*, on the subject of sex discrimination at the upper reaches of the legal profession.

Other subjects that you might consider include family care and client relations. For example, how should women (and men for that matter) handle the client who must take second place to a sick child? Do you tell him the whole truth — or something less? These problems are not overwhelming but may seem so to the associate involved. Like other mundane matters — such as time sheets, billing, and conflicts of interest — they can be treated in an hour or two of training that will improve efficiency and morale and avoid embarrassing incidents.

Your Summer Clerks May Be Getting Better Training Than Your Associates

Each year, as the foliage begins to turn and the breezes freshen, your summer clerks trickle off to more languid pursuits or they return to stuffy law review offices. Before the memories of your most recent summer program dim, you should examine them to develop useful insights into your entire firm training program.

Summer clerks learn in three ways about a firm's commitment to lawyer training. First, a firm may provide them with an occasional training workshop as a welcome diversion from the traditional social outings and athletic contests. Second, summer clerks will get more than a little sense of the firm's commitment to training from the kind of supervision, feedback, and counseling received over the summer. And third, of course, your summer clerks will gossip with your permanent associates.

Formal training programs for summer clerks are not widespread. Some firms simply don't want to spend the money on outside instructors or ask their partners to prepare elaborate in-house sessions for summer clerks. Why, they argue, should we do more than we are already to finance their legal training? We pay them plenty, and we won't reap the benefits of training most of them because they will end up at other firms. Furthermore, training summer clerks in skills like trial advocacy or negotiation is impractical because there's no way they will use these skills until well into their full-time post-law school careers. By then, they will have forgotten anything they might have learned during the summer. Let them sit in on departmental seminars and the like. But otherwise, they should spend office time trying to earn their outrageous pay with a little honest work doing research, one of the few things they may have been trained to do in law school.

These arguments are credible. But they are not convincing. The financial obstacle is the least convincing. Most firms spend more on parties and theater tickets than they could possibly invest in outside instructors for summer training workshops. And we know that students are far more likely to remember a useful legal writing or negotiating workshop than another country club outing. Even if your summer trainees do end up joining other firms, you will benefit. The campus reputation of your law firm is more likely to be enhanced by good word of mouth about your summer training program than about your social calendar.

Sure, students between their first and second year of law school are not likely to put most practical skills to immediate use. But if you don't help them with their writing and editing, they are unlikely to learn these skills in law school. Law schools do have writing programs, but most of them are useless at best and retrograde at worst. After all, who teaches them? Law professors generally don't write well. And many law schools fulfill their obligation to teach writing with deadly courses headed by teaching fellows with no particular background or interest in writing. Similarly, litigation training or a workshop in negotiating may be more useful than you think if the students are going to spend some time in a law school clinical program. Thus the few firms that have offered short courses in these subjects have had good results.

But summer training programs have a value beyond the possibility that students may be able to put these techniques to immediate use. In a highly effective way, these programs demonstrate what lawyers do when they grow up. Almost always, summer clerks come to me after a negotiating workshop and report that they now understand the difference between "knowing" real estate law, for example, and making deals. All of a sudden, they realize that lawyering requires knowledge and training to be sure, but it also requires working closely with clients, making deals, and helping people stay out of or get out of trouble. These tasks are far more satisfying — and more fun — than the intellectual exercises that law students perform in law school.

Some firms include permanent associates and even partners in their summer negotiating workshops. The result is somewhere in between a country club outing and a deadly serious training program. Like a country club outing, summer recruits get to see partners in a different, informal setting. But they also get to see partners and permanent associates display their skills and vulnerabilities. If your firm's lawyers have sufficiently strong egos, such sessions can be useful, memorable, and fun.

Supervising and mentoring summer clerks are more traditional ways of handling them, however, than formal training programs. And, ironically, many firms have discovered that their supervision of summer clerks is more successful than that of year-round lawyers. When this happens it's usually the result of the greater care and attention given to assigning work, overseeing it, and providing feedback. Too many firms provide no workable means to assure that permanent associates receive assignments that will broaden and deepen their experience. Yet some of these same firms painstakingly set up elaborate work assignment systems for the summer program. More important, the hiring committee, or some other attentive management group, makes damn sure the system works.

And summer clerks usually get work from the partners who have the interest and ability to supervise effectively. Assignments are likely to be explained with care. Regular opportunities for consultation and review are established. Feedback is delivered promptly. In several firms, partners are told that if they do not follow through on assignments to summer clerks, no more summer clerks will be assigned to them.

Of course, painstaking attention is paid to summer clerks because you must evaluate them to decide whether to make offers. Also, they are evaluating you, and you want them to do so favorably and accept your offers.

But while everyone acknowledges the need for mutual evaluation in summer programs, few see the even greater need to evaluate permanent associates to determine whether, how, and at what rate they should advance in the firm. You have a far greater investment in permanent associates than in summer clerks. And, these days, permanent associates who are any good are likely to be scouted by headhunters. So you have an even stronger interest in keeping them happy than in entertaining your summer clerks. Nothing is more costly to a law firm than to suffer excessive turnover of associates at the two- to three-year level, just when they may be turning into profit centers.

Summer clerks are more likely than permanent associates to be taken along to court, meetings with clients, and negotiations. Somehow the same firms that fear client backlash from "over-lawyering" with full-time lawyers overcome their apprehensions in the interests of recruiting. These firms may counter that clients understand that summer clerks are there for the learning experience. That's right. And the same clients can be informed that permanent associates need such learning experiences, too.

In-house training gossip is the last, and perhaps definitive, way for summer clerks to learn about your training policies. No matter the number of cruises on the Potomac, tickets to *Cats*, or

exciting work assignments, summer clerks will talk to permanent associates. And that's how their impressions of your firm
are molded. If your commitment to training stops on Labor Day
and excludes your full-time lawyers, you can't hide that fact
behind a glittering summer schedule.

What are your permanent associates telling your summer
clerks? If they are saying that assignments are made hap-
hazardly and supervision is hard to come by, your superior
summer training program will be considered no more meaningful than the social events that dwindle down when law
graduates join the firm permanently. If permanent associates
lament that their only feedback comes when they screw up in
some massive way and that their periodic evaluations tell them
nothing, summer clerks will be unlikely to join up, even if you
lay on a workshop in writing and editing and tickets to see Bruce
Springsteen.

If you have a good summer training program, it's time to
examine it closely and apply the lessons learned to your entire
firm. These days lawyers know they can't compete for top law
graduates without an effective summer program. But neither
can you hope to get your more important permanent associates
up to speed and keep them with you unless you offer them an
equally effective training program.

Library Staff Can
Play a Useful Lawyer
Training Role

Foot doctors have become podiatrists, old folks are now senior citizens, and librarians are beginning to call themselves information specialists. Whether the first two transformations serve any useful social purpose is beyond me, but we lawyers *can* benefit from thinking about the implications of the last name change. Librarians, as we all know, shelve books and keep pocket parts up to date. But perhaps information specialists can play a new role in lawyer training.

Lawyers need three kinds of knowledge: cognitive information, practical skills, and understanding, or wisdom. The second and third are sexier than the first. My attention is mainly devoted to teaching skills, because firms are usually most perplexed about how to do it.

But the stodgy truth is that most of what we need to know is cognitive information. John Adams and Abraham Lincoln picked it up reading law by candlelight. And reading is still our most efficient learning mode. Books, periodicals, and advance sheets contain most of the cognitive information we need, if only our briefcases were big enough to carry it all around and there were enough free hours in the day to read it. Librarians, however, who may not be skilled in specific legal specialities, *are* trained to sense what resources are worth our time. At a minimum, therefore, encourage your library staff to share with your lawyers what is being published. Good librarians should be able to screen the stuff and keep lawyers from wasting their time on publications that are obviously trash.

Librarians also know how to do research — or at least they

know where various materials can be located. You certainly can't assume that law students are prepared to do research in the law you are currently practicing. In the fall of 1984 I heard Harvard law professor Milton Katz admit to our 20th-reunion class that Harvard courses — and by extrapolation other law schools' courses — are consistently 15 to 20 years behind the practice of law. He looked at Harvard catalogs dating back to the nineteenth century and discovered that Harvard ignored the antitrust laws for at least 15 years, avoided any consistent effort to teach taxation for a generation after the income tax became a permanent fact of life, didn't catch on to corporate law for a similar period, and failed to teach securities law until the 1950s.

Thus your firm is likely to be practicing some relatively arcane law that poses research challenges to your associates. Computer law, space law, Indian law, and the interface of law and technology are unlikely to have been taught in law school.

But librarians can train lawyers in research skills. Shearman & Sterling, for example, incorporates into its associate orientation program esoteric research problems for which librarians can be a valuable training resource. Library staff should offer an orientation program to fully acquaint new lawyers with your library facilities.

You are probably using some on-line research tools. Lawyers are using not only LEXIS and Westlaw but also NEXIS and Dialog, on-line data bases that include newspapers, magazines, scholarly journals, and professional publications in fields far removed from the law itself. Now they can also use AMBAR which is the American Bar Association's data base. (Now if only the ABA would improve its ratio of good material to insipid fluff.)

But in many firms, librarians do on-line research themselves, especially when the material is not conventionally law-related because lawyers too often don't know enough about extralegal on-line data bases. However, librarians can't be expected to home in on the subject as precisely as the lawyer responsible for the matter.

If they don't already, you should beseech your librarians to run data base training programs, or to schedule such programs with outside trainers from the data base services themselves. And if you're really smart and want to increase your firm's use of computers, you'll further exploit your library staff's knowledge. Chances are they know more about computers than any other department in your firm. After all, computers are information banks, and librarians are information specialists.

Librarians thus may be the best trainers of lawyers and paralegals who should begin to utilize computers for spreadsheet analysis, case management data retrieval, project management, editing, and even word processing. Your librarians may want to enlist some secretaries in the effort too, because the greatest barrier between lawyers and computers is probably a lack of typing skills. (This mystifies me, because I only have for certain retained one skill acquired in grammar school and that is typing.) They may also want to call in psychologists, because some lawyers seem to think that their images will be shattered if they are seen using typewriter keyboards.

Even if you reject all of the proposals outlined so far, I beg you to enlist your information specialists in organizing and making accessible your form files. Law firms with organized, current form files are rarer than states that went to Mondale in 1984. Associates have enough to learn about the practice of law without having to learn that the best forms for the pleadings they must draft are in your bottom right-hand drawer, under the Reese's Pieces. Professional librarians know how to collect, catalog, and maintain data, and putting your form files in order may make them heroes and heroines in your office. In a short time, your productivity will improve dramatically. And if your library staff becomes overworked, increase their numbers: after all, you should expect to spend more on information specialists than on librarians.

You can derive yet another training benefit from the collection and maintenance of your forms and checklists. Associates can be regularly assigned to update and revise these forms, and the sessions at which senior and junior lawyers review the proposed updates will be some of the most productive and least expensive training experiences you will have.

Videotape libraries are another area in which your librarians may be able to save you money. No doubt many of you are beginning to purchase CLE videotapes. Have you turned this job over to your librarians? Think about it. Among other things, they may be able to collaborate with their colleagues in other firms and legal departments to organize a videotape collective.

Even good videotapes are used infrequently, and given their relatively steep price, it makes little sense for even the largest firms to buy tapes that will spend most of the year gathering dust on shelves. However, a well-maintained collective will allow you to share not only the tapes but formal or informal reviews of them, as well as suggestions for editing to get the most out of the tapes and avoid the worst.

In addition to shifting some training responsibilities to your library staff, you can shift some of the budget their way too. One way to keep at bay partners who are skeptical of the costs of training is to fool them — benignly, of course — by shifting some training costs to the library budget. If you are caught, you can easily defend your decision. Just be certain that your librarians remember to hide this book.

In-House Training Within Smaller Firms

The conventional wisdom is that formal in-house training programs are beyond the means of smaller firms. Of course, Paul, Hastings, Janofsky & Walker, Shearman & Sterling, Baker & McKenzie, Morrison & Foerster, and the U.S. Department of Justice — organizations with hundreds of lawyers and scores of new recruits each year — can and should mount their own formal training programs. But firms of 50, or 25, or 10 lawyers cannot be expected to follow suit.

The conventional wisdom is wrong. In fact, small law firms, even the smallest, ought to create their own training programs because not only can they muster the necessary resources, they need such training programs even more than big firms.

Small firms can use training programs to compensate for their inevitable structural and organizational problems. The biggest law firms can afford the luxury of long-term apprenticeships for new lawyers: work can easily be apportioned among lawyers with varying levels of skill and experience. But in small firms, lawyers with relatively little seniority are often assigned their own legal matters. They are likely not only to practice more law than their large-firm counterparts but to be supervised less.

Associates in big firms may not see a client for years, so there is little reason to train them in client interviewing and counseling. If they go to court at all, they will be assigned insignificant cases, or they will be second-stringers on large litigation teams. Small-firm associates, however, may very well be interviewing and counseling clients within a few months of admission to the bar. They are more likely to be thrown into trials for which **109** they've had little experience and will receive even less supervision. Perhaps the bad reviews litigators have recently gotten from the Chief Justice and others arise in part from this phenomenon.

All lawyers are busy, but resources are typically thinner in small firms than in big ones. Senior lawyers in small firms can't afford the time it takes to edit or rewrite the unacceptable drafts of inexperienced lawyers. Nor can they afford to hire editors.

Thus formal skills training programs are important in smaller firms, to ensure that they offer competent service to their clients and fulfill the ethical requirement of Rule 1.1 of the new ABA Model Rules of Professional Conduct that "A lawyer shall provide competent representation to a client." But there are other reasons as well: few smaller firms can compete economically in the zany process of recruitment because salaries and perquisites in the big firms are almost always on a grander scale. Sensible job candidates, though, will look favorably on the smaller firm that offers a first-class training program. Solid, systematic preparation for a life in the legal profession is worth a lot to them. It's worth considerably more than the incremental salary advantage offered by a giant firm with little interest in offering broad training in a range of specialities to its recruits, many of whom will never become partners.

Most big firms are highly specialized, but sometimes profess a cohesiveness among their departments that is more wishful thinking than fact. Smaller firms can achieve this cohesiveness if they develop lawyers who care about the firm as a whole, regardless of their specialties. General orientation programs and interdepartmental training seminars and workshops can help smaller firms achieve the high degree of cohesiveness they want and need.

Of course, smaller firms don't need formal training programs if they have none of these problems. And, you may argue, means other than formal training programs — such as departmental rotation and good on-the-job training — can overcome these problems. Smaller firms, however, are less likely than their bigger cousins to use these alternative means. Although rotation and close supervision of new lawyers — as we will see below — can be effective components of an in-house training program, there are inherent problems. A rotation system for new associates, for example, is likely to be inefficient in the smaller firm, where the departure of an associate from one department may cripple it, while his arrival in another may not coincide with the arrival of sufficient work. Or even if there is work aplenty in his new department, it may not be diverse enough to provide the range and depth of experience that you and he both desire.

An informal system of supervision is also likely to disintegrate under the stress of small-firm practice. Supervisors often believe that it's more efficient to do low-level work themselves because they can do it faster and better than their assistants. When they assign work to newer lawyers, they have problems finding time to review it with them in an instructive way. And even when there is time, supervisors may not be good teachers for lack of training or inclination.

Yet in-house training is available to all lawyers who want it: even one-and two-person firms can undertake many programs. Theirs might depend heavily on the new technology, especially audio and videotapes, which are widely available. Litigation skills, for example, are intensively covered in model trials, demonstrations, and how-to-do-it workshops available on videotape from a large number of producers, including the National Institute for Trial Advocacy, the American Bar Association, Video-Law, and the Practising Law Institute. Videotapes are also available to help you develop other lawyering skills, including client interviewing, counseling, and negotiation. Best-selling author Herb Cohen has a series of negotiating videotapes available from Magnetic Video, PLI publishes another set of negotiating tapes, and the ABA Consortium for Professional Education has released tapes on client interviewing and counseling. With these materials, one-and two-person firms can save considerable time and money and create their own training schedules.

Programs presenting substantive information on the law are also widely available on video and audiotape; in fact, in-house training can even become "in-car" training with CLE audio tapes. One novel method of keeping up has been developed by ALI-ABA which put CLE "magazines" on audiotape.

Nor are the smallest firms limited to high-tech programs. Conscientious small-firm lawyers can and do retain training consultants to help sharpen their written and oral communication skills. It's also possible to organize a consortium of small firms with similar goals to develop training programs as elaborate as any big firm's.

Clinical-type training workshops are, in fact, well suited to small firms because the best hands-on training workshops are limited in size, usually to 10 or 15 lawyers. Training programs that attempt to reach a larger group amount to no more than lectures. If the group is kept small, however, effective hands-on training can take place. Writing programs, for example, can focus on the actual writing of each participant, and instructors can spend some time with each in individual tutorial sessions. Negotiation can be taught by means of simulations and demonstrations in which every participant has the opportunity to perform.

Even in the biggest firms, such training efforts must be **111** targeted at small groups. For example, Joel Henning & Associates generally restricts participation in writing workshops to 15 lawyers. Big organizations that want to include more participants must do so by offering several workshops consecutively or sequentially.

If training programs make sense for small firms, why don't more have them? In most cases, the problem is not money — or should not be — because successful training programs are cost-effective, particularly in an era of high associate salaries and overhead. It stands to reason then that a program that accelerates associates' full performance as lawyers will justify reasonable expenditures.

More often the problem is time. The pace is terribly fast in successful small firms. Partners so beleaguered that they do their own research and writing rather than take the time to assign it to an assistant who must be supervised are also too busy to plan a systematic training program. Like so many other projects, training remains on the back burner — something that small firms would like to do but defer until there is more time. But there never is "more time," there is only less time.

Despite the obvious problems that confront the small firm desiring to create a training program, it can be done. But without the total commitment of your firm's partners, it will probably never get off the ground. A successful case in point is Boothe, Prichard & Dudley of McLean, Virginia, a firm of approximately 65 lawyers. Boothe, Prichard first established its goal: to "provide our clients with timely and high-quality legal service through the recruitment, training and retention of highly qualified and motivated lawyers." The firm then created an associate training program managed by a committee of all its department heads who, with others, offer in-house seminars and lectures.

They have also profoundly enriched the firm's supervisory and rotation programs. Each Boothe, Prichard associate is systematically supervised by a partner, some on a daily basis. But because the associates are not necessarily doing the work of their supervisors, some of the problems discussed above are avoided. The supervisors, who can be a little more detached than is usual, closely supervise the associate's performance and report periodically to the associate's department head.

To transform the departmental rotation program into a more useful training experience, Boothe, Prichard's litigation, business, and land departments each prepared an elaborate "Associate Task List." Each list sets out in detail the work that an associate must do while assigned to a department.

For example, the business department's task list includes work in real estate, business entities, quasi-public bodies, financial institutions, securities, workouts, and several other areas. The litigation department requires each associate to handle five trials as sole counsel in general district court; five unlawful detainer cases; become familiar with the firm's docket-keeping process; attend at least two term days in state circuit court; handle 10 motions and demurrers; assist in several discovery matters; handle the discovery phases of five cases; assist in preparing and trying five cases; at least four of which are before juries; and to prepare and try himself five cases, at least four of which are before juries. Litigation associates must also handle several motions in federal district court and perform other tasks leading up to the preparation and trial of three cases that the associate handles himself. Associates assigned to the land section undertake tasks under 15 separate areas of practice, ranging from subdivision documents to foreclosure sales.

Associates participate in the Boothe, Prichard training program for three years. During that period, they receive no bonuses. Instead, Boothe, Prichard invests in the training program the funds that would otherwise have been awarded as bonuses. Moreover, Boothe, Prichard lawyers believe their training program to be a powerful recruiting tool.

The Boothe, Prichard program is both elaborate and effective. Because it was designed specifically for Boothe, Prichard, it would not necessarily work for any other firm; however, it serves as a dramatic example that — so long as the entire partnership supports the effort — smaller firms can develop a comprehensive training program.

Indeed, the worst mistake a small firm can make is to attempt a training program that does not suit it. You may decide you can do it entirely on your own, or you may decide to seek outside services in planning or implementation. But whichever you decide on, don't forget you chose to practice law in a small firm — in particular, your small firm. Make certain the training program you develop trades on your strengths, not the strengths of another small firm, and certainly not the strengths of a big one.

If you can establish a program as unique as your firm, you can also enhance the qualities of the firm you helped to build, and your firm's prospects will be brighter.

Teaching Clinical Skills

The clinical approach to teaching lawyering skills bears little relationship to conventional continuing legal education. CLE usually involves expository teaching — lectures and panel discussions. But clinical skills teaching is more like tennis camp than conventional CLE: the objective is not to impart cognitive information but to sharpen practical skills.

Tennis camps and clinical teaching of lawyering skills use many of the same techniques. Both require extensive student participation. Both call for frequent demonstrations by experts. Both use videotape replays to show students how they performed. Both require instructors to watch student performances thoroughly and critique them constructively, carefully balancing positive and negative feedback to maximize students' progress. Most important, neither tennis camp nor the clinical teaching of lawyering skills benefit from instructors lapsing into the lecture mode. The clinical learning process depends upon simulation and critique. These methods should be intimately related, but that relationship breaks down when anecdotes, lectures, and "war stories" intervene.

For both faculty and students, teaching through simulation and critique is intensive. Unlike lectures which can be designed in advance, even written out word for word, clinical teaching cannot. The student performance and the faculty critique require substantial preparation, but neither can ever be fully orchestrated in advance. This unpredictability, though stimulating, is also difficult because workshops are necessarily of limited duration. All simulations and critiques must be con-

115

densed, and very few can be carried to completion even in that condensed form.

Keep in mind that clinical teaching is best done on two levels. One could be called "public." During class sessions, comments and critiques should be applicable to all students present. But faculty should also find time to meet privately with students to review videotapes of their simulations and critique the problems unique to individual students.

Perhaps most important for faculty to remember is that students should be allowed to struggle, but not to fail. If, during a simulation, a student encounters a problem related to substantive law it is often best to interrupt and provide the necessary information quickly. If, however, a student is struggling because of a skill-related problem, the instructor must use judgment in deciding how long to let the struggle continue. Don't let a student continue until he or she utterly fails. Interrupt the simulation after a minute or so and provide help. If the student seems incapable of continuing, terminate the simulation.

Before class, faculty can best prepare by working through the case problems for the day as if they were students. They might outline an approach, including topics to be covered, questions to raise, problems likely to come up, and alternative ways of dealing with them.

But no one can offer the definitive teaching method: lawyering is an art, not a science. Different instructors, many of them practicing lawyers, will prefer different approaches. Moreover, differences of opinion among instructors should be encouraged, so long as debates are not protracted. Students should understand that several approaches and techniques can achieve the same objective. Allow students to choose for themselves those most likely to work for them. Disagreements among faculty that enhance this objective are useful; those directed only to winning the argument obviously are not.

You will find that there is never enough time. Student performances must be cut off, critiques must be abridged. Students and faculty must understand that this shortness of time means the course will be intensive and stressful, much like lawyering itself. Don't try to eliminate stress, but don't let it get out of hand either.

Give all students equal time to perform. While some imbalances are inevitable, the team leader in each sequence must take responsibility for alloting more or less equal time to each student performance and, similarly, for critiquing each student's performance in a roughly equal way.

Observing and critiquing a student performance is an art, but some of the following suggestions may be useful. Many clinical instructors find it helpful to keep a pad of paper in front of them. Draw a line down the middle of the page, and during student performances maintain a rough transcript of the dialogue on one side of the paper. On the other side, make brief notes for the critiquing session. This system helps instructors to be specific with students during the critiques. Actual dialogue can be cited in relation to the element to be discussed.

Be specific about positive as well as negative aspects of the students' performances. If a certain technique did not work well discuss what would have worked, as well as what did not. Occasionally the best way to indicate a successful tactic in place of one that failed is to demonstrate it. Students appreciate role models and respect instructors willing and able to perform themselves as well as to criticize.

An effective critique contains several elements. Obviously you should address the objectives which the student had in mind. Another element involves the student's tactics, and a third, his or her style. Team leaders may find it helpful to assign an individual faculty member to observe and critique each element. Team leaders should also be responsible for ensuring that no one faculty member monopolizes a critique (unless this method is planned on and agreed to in advance) and for encouraging students to participate constructively in the critiques of others.

Videotape is critically important to clinical teaching in at least three ways. First, tapes of model demonstrations can be prepared in advance for use at various points in the course.

Second, videotape can be used to record a student's performance and offer an "instant replay" of it. Some instructors play back each student videotape in full immediately after the role playing. Often students do not believe they did or said something until they witness it on tape. The critique can be woven throughout the videotape replay, which can be stopped as often as seems appropriate. Other instructors use the student videotapes selectively to illustrate certain points during the critiquing sessions following role playing. With a little practice and coordination with the video technicians, specific points in the tape can quickly be found.

Whichever method you choose, don't forget the third important videotape technique. Students must have ample opportunity to watch their individual videotapes privately, with an instructor present. This critiquing session can and should differ substantially from regular class sessions. Instructors can criticize many elements of a student's performance that would be embarrassing and counterproductive to mention during classroom sessions. Furthermore, students can and will ask questions of instructors in private that they would not ask during class. Evaluations of our own past programs have indicated that students really wanted adequate time to review their own videotapes in private, with the helpful advice of the instructor. **117**

Finally, a note on role playing. Most students not only enjoy it but find it to be an effective learning technique. A few students, however, find role playing difficult. Some have never been in training programs using this technique, and they may be uncomfortable about being asked to "pretend." They may express a general discomfort and reluctance to participate in role playing. Underlying this anxiety, however, we have found that the student is usually apprehensive about his or her ability to perform well in front of peers.

Rarely does a class of 24 have more than a couple of students who have difficulties with role playing. Where this problem does occur, use discretion. To overcome students' reluctance, consider a role-playing demonstration by the instructors. Don't give up on role-playing. It is essential and cannot be avoided. Finally, be sensitive to students' level of competence. For example, you might put your weaker students on first so that you do not intimidate them with superstar performances.

When it's all over, you are almost certain to have enjoyed the experience, and your students will have, too. Try it. You'll like it.

Supervising and Mentoring Younger Lawyers

Stop Talking About Supervisory Skills and Do Something About Them

> When you want to persuade somebody to do something, you have to show them.... You learn by looking, not by talking.... Jacques [D'Amboise]... comes to me and says, "Tell me, what do you think is wrong with this?" He feels it's not right but doesn't know why. "Well, first of all, you stay too long in diagonal.... Why don't you shorten it and make it this way, forget this and that, OK, and hit that little dip?"... So it becomes a little better, and then he likes it.
>
> George Balanchine

George Balanchine created the most accomplished ballet company in the United States. But in a fascinating *New Yorker* interview published after his death, Balanchine insists that the New York City Ballet was just another dance company until his own affiliated ballet school fully matured. "Now we don't audition professional dancers. We take just from the school. And the school gives our style, also because the [students] now participate in performances; they are ready. They are part of it."

Balanchine's ballet company can serve in many respects as a role model for law firms. His own career serves as an example of how skilled practitioners can be teachers. The key in dancing and lawyering is carefully supervised on-the-job training.

Why is a good law firm more like a good ballet company than like a General Motors assembly plant? GM supervisors are responsible for work flow, quality control, and safety. So, to some extent, are ballet directors and law firm partners. But in the dance and law worlds, the supervisor's most important role is to teach, to impart the requisite skills to the next generation. Whereas workers on an assembly line are unlikely to move up within their organization, in a ballet company or a law firm the best talent will rise. And that talent will perpetuate and enhance the institution. If it doesn't rise, the institution will die. One of Balanchine's greatest achievements was developing dancers like Peter Martins and Jacques D'Amboise so that they could take over. Martins became co-ballet master in chief of the New York City Ballet shortly before Balanchine's death in 1983.

Lingering for a moment in the rarified world of ballet, we can find one more useful point. Balanchine could dance brilliantly, choreograph imaginatively, *and* develop his company, but to do it all simultaneously, the critics said, was his genius. Yet all senior lawyers — even those who are less than geniuses — must do the equivalent. It's not easy — something like being a successful baseball player-manager, of which there are notably few in the major leagues.

So what else is new, you might say. All major firms recognize the need for careful supervisors and helpful mentors. The problem is that they recognize the need and pay it homage, but few firms do much to insure that the need is fulfilled. More than half the lawyers who responded to a 1985 ABA survey said they were not happy in their jobs, and one reason cited was the lack of feedback and training.

There are several fundamental reasons why lawyers have trouble fulfilling their supervisory roles. First, human beings generally resist criticizing one another (except for their spouses). What's worse, they also ignore opportunities to praise one another (especially their spouses). Associates often do not hear a word from their supervising partners. They don't know whether they have succeeded or failed on a project unless they hear indirectly of a happy partner or a satisfied client. It's so easy to give praise, but so often we don't offer it when due.

Second, there's the lonesome cowboy syndrome in the law. We consider ourselves to be resolutely independent professionals relating to one another more like fourteenth-century feudal barons than like members of a Marine platoon under enemy fire. Our dislike of being told what to do somehow weakens our ability to instruct others. Oh, sure, we can make assignments, but we'd rather correct the errors ourselves than criticize the associate who made them. Senior lawyers often go to the extreme of redoing an associate's work rather than providing that associate with the feedback he or she needs to revise it. As a result, the senior lawyer too often performs low-level research and drafting — an inefficient use of his time. And the junior lawyer does not improve at the maximum possible rate because he or she is not being constructively criticized.

Third, law firms increasingly include women and people of different ethnic and geographic backgrounds. And the general reluctance to criticize is aggravated when the criticism might be misinterpreted as an ethnic slur or a sexist attack. In 1982, two Wellesley professors studied women professionals and discovered they were advancing more slowly than their male counterparts. The women surveyed did not believe themselves to be the victims of conscious discrimination; rather, they felt that their male supervisors were giving them less feedback and training. Their supervisors' reticence arose out of discomfort and unfamiliarity, not out of prejudice, but the results were the same. Similarly, Kay Bridger-Riley has reported that when she became the first woman associate to join an Omaha law firm the partners' efforts to avoid any hint of discrimination also meant they didn't provide the negative feedback that would have helped her develop more quickly.

A good supervisor usually has two roles — traffic cop and teacher. As traffic cop, the supervisor must control the work flow and review work product to insure that it meets the firm's quality standards. These elements of supervision apply equally to the GM assembly line supervisor, the ballet master, or lawyer. They are less romantic aspects of supervision than teaching. But if work assignments and quality control are not handled efficiently, the supervisor and the supervisee cannot develop an effective teacher-student relationship. Conversely, a supervisor's success as a teacher will minimize the time he or she must spend on the managerial aspects of supervision.

The supervisor's role as traffic cop in the modern law firm or legal department is more complicated than it used to be. In the days of slow, stable growth, only a few new lawyers were brought in each year. In most firms, there were enough skilled, interested senior lawyers to take the new recruits in hand, often on a one-on-one basis. But today — whether they welcome the assignment or not — senior lawyers are often responsible for a multitude of associates. Some of these senior lawyers find that it's all they can do to allocate work flow and review important documents before they leave the office.

The supervisor as teacher is the more glamorous, but more difficult role. We all know that the best practitioners are not necessarily the best teachers. For example, there is a big difference between writing elegantly oneself and being an effective legal writing coach. That's why many good lawyers would rather rewrite the tatty first-draft brief than carefully review it with the perpetrating associate and give him or her another crack at it.

One often-neglected fact of life is that supervision deserves regular attention. If your law firm is to prosper, supervisory skills are desperately important. No amount of in-house training or CLE seminars can overcome inadequate supervision of day-to-day work assignments. But most lawyers I meet tell me privately that only a few of their colleagues seem to devote to supervision the time and attention it requires.

Why is something so important so often done badly or not at all? The first response I usually get is that good supervision takes time, and today's competitive practice of law does not afford such time. But time sheets, monthly billing, lawyer recruiting, and other aspects of law firm management also take time. Up until now, however, only a few firms have recognized that time devoted to supervision is at least as important as time committed to these other responsibilities.

We must stop talking about good supervision and do something about it. One possible change in firm policy — perhaps the only meaningful change — would alter the reward system to recognize good supervision: you would pay lawyers more for being good supervisors, and less for ignoring their supervisory responsibilities. Of course this policy change would cause a furor among partners. But were there not similar furors over the steps you took to insure that recalcitrant partners turned in time sheets regularly and billed their clients monthly?

Of course, one fundamental difference divides new policies affecting cash flow from those intended to improve supervision. The ability to supervise subordinates is a skill and, like other essential lawyering skills, it must be learned. Some senior lawyers will be better at it than others, but these skills can also be taught to some extent. The next chapter discusses techniques for improving supervisory skills.

How to Be a Better Mentor and Supervisor of Lawyers

In the last chapter I attempted to explain why supervising young lawyers is so important, yet so often done badly. And because lawyers ought to stop talking about good supervision and do something about it, in this chapter I'll try to give you a few tips on supervision.

First, let's distinguish a supervisor from a mentor. A supervisor assigns and oversees the work of subordinate lawyers. But overseeing in this case includes coaching, tutoring, teaching, criticizing, and evaluating. And as discussed in the last chapter, oversight of lawyers is different than oversight of assembly line workers. The assembly line foreman cares mainly about productivity, quality control, and perhaps safety. Neither he nor the workers on the line expect upward mobility. Obviously expectations are very different in a law firm. Your subordinates fully expect to move up the hierarchy — if not in your firm, then somewhere else. For the future of your firm and of your supervisee, you can't be merely a foreman.

On the other hand, a true supervisor cannot simultaneously be a mentor. By definition, a mentor is a wise and trusted counselor. And it's not reasonable if you are assigning, criticizing, and evaluating as a supervisor, to expect your supervisee to also seek you out for wisdom and counsel. Occasionally a supervisor becomes a mentor (as in the case of William Agee and Mary Cunningham). But don't count on it happening naturally. The two relationships are necessarily different, and that's not a bad thing.

So split up these functions in your firm. Associates will benefit **125** from access to mentors who are not at all responsible for their day-to-day work. Moreover, supervisors and mentors can teach different things.

As Mortimer Adler reminds us in his recent critique of American public education, *The Paideia Proposal*, people (including lawyers) improve their minds in three different ways: the acquisition of organized knowledge; the development of intellectual skills; and the enlargement of understanding, insight, and common sense.

Each of these learning modes demands different teaching techniques. Lawyers can often pick up organized knowledge relatively easily, through textbooks, legal encyclopedias, forms, advance sheets, and external or in-house CLE lectures. Certainly supervisors and mentors need not waste their limited time on lecturing. But you should help associates find the right books, forms, advance sheets, and CLE courses.

The supervisor's principal role as teacher should involve the second learning mode — skills development. Lectures won't accelerate the development of lawyering skills such as writing, negotiating, counseling, and litigating. But on-the-job coaching and supervising will, and simulated exercises will. Remember, every time you personally rewrite an associate's unacceptable draft and send it out, offering no feedback to the draftsperson, you abandon your responsibilities as a supervisor. You may save time in the short term, but you are not investing in your firm's or the associate's future. By the same token, don't fail to bring your supervisee along when you negotiate merely because you can't justify 100 percent billing for his or her time. If necessary, set aside some occasions when you won't bill at all, or bill at a lesser rate, acknowledging the training factor.

And when there simply isn't enough time for careful and detailed on-the-job coaching, in-house skills training workshops, based on simulated cases and other matters, can achieve some of the same objectives. If you have neither the time nor the expertise, of course you can bring in consultants, but in-house skills workshops get better results if your partners participate as instructors or coaches. In other words, you can't totally buy your way out of your training responsibilities.

That leaves open the question of how to teach young lawyers good judgment, insight, and common sense. Some senior lawyers roll their eyes skyward and insist the task is hopeless. But this is where a good mentoring relationship can pay big dividends. These elusive qualities of mind can be taught, says Adler, through dialogue and discussion. I won't call this the Socratic method, partly because we instantly picture John Houseman badgering 150 law students in a lecture hall. In fact, Socrates was at his best in an intimate (often *extremely* intimate) dialogue, one student at a time. He was more a mentor than a

Harvard law professor.

Mentors can also socialize new lawyers, integrating them into the profession and the firm. In the law, largely an adversarial process, we are supposed to represent our clients zealously. Nevertheless, the profession is also a nexus of strong and subtle relationships — among lawyers in the same firm (as well as paralegals and secretaries), adversaries, courts and other government agencies, the organized bar, and clients. The way we handle these relationships is not obvious to new lawyers. But they will more quickly learn the ropes with the help of wise and trusted mentors.

Of course, good supervision takes time — but make time. Many of your partners assume that any hours not billed are wasted — including the time spent developing junior lawyers. These partners are not only wrong, they will lead your firm to extinction, and here's why.

Every lawyer should be a profit center. In the olden days, he who billed the most hours was the most profitable because corporate law was based on a kind of "cost-plus" billing system. If the general counsel of ABC Corporation asked you to try a case, or register a securities offering, or close an acquisition, you billed at a rate that met your overhead and assured you a handsome profit. Thus the cost-plus system typically allowed you to pass on the cost of your firm's inefficiencies to the ABC Corporation.

Those days are gone. Corporations now understand that they can purchase legal services much as they do other goods, scouting out the best product at the lowest price. In other words, now you will pay for your firm's inefficiencies. And an untrained associate is bound to be inefficient. So the resources you fail to invest in supervision and training will come back to haunt you: the new economics will not reward the firm that bills every waking minute of every partner and associate, but rather the firm that offers the best product in the most efficient way, at the lowest cost.

Sure, coaching and supervision take some time that can't be billed. But the time spent supervising will be rewarded when the supervisee becomes a more efficient lawyer or, in the parlance of the ubiquitous cost accountant, a profit center.

So taking the time is important — but also make sure it's the *right* time and place. Too much supervision goes on in the corridors: "That was a good memo, Sally. Good work." Or: "I asked for a four-page draft and you gave me 30 pages of drivel." Obviously you don't want to deliver feedback that begins and ends with just such brief comments delivered publicly any more than you would counsel your client in an elevator. When you initiate a supervisory relationship, be explicit about your expectations and solicit those of your supervisee. Make clear **127** which projects you want done fast, without coaching or feed-back, and which you will carefully review.

It's a common failing to give the follow-up too late. Six months after a project is finished, an associate will not recall in detail what he or she did. What's worse, other work in the months intervening will probably, and unnecessarily, suffer from the same feelings. If the first critique a project receives is during an annual performance review, you are being profoundly unfair to your associate.

If your firm has a good form for evaluating associates or prospective partners, perhaps you'll want to focus on its criteria for success as you coach your supervisors. If you don't have such a form, develop one.

Set up a regular time for meetings, even if you sometimes have to change it. Early morning sessions work well (if you're both early morning people). Lunchtime may be convenient and it minimizes the need for either of you to curtail billable hours. Lunches, however, should perhaps be in a small conference room rather than in a club or restaurant where you can't spread out your drafts, forms, and books. The end of the day is not usually a good time: supervisors and supervisees may be exhausted or nervous about train schedules and dinner prep-arations. Supervisory sessions scheduled for the end of the day often just don't happen.

You know how important your clients are — but your de-veloping associates are no less important. When you try a case or negotiate a deal, you prepare. You decide what's important and what's not important. You get organized. You develop a strategy. The same kind of planning should precede your supervisory sessions.

For example, when you edit an associate's brief, you may alter his or her draft to the last stylistic idiosyncrasy. That's fine if the brief is going out under your name. But don't waste limited supervisory time on what may be your compulsive habits of style. Concentrate instead on the associate's fundamental weaknesses, perhaps of clarity, precision, persuasiveness, or organization, and on how well he or she grasps the essence of the case.

And don't forget the associate's strengths. Positive feedback usually comes a lot easier, but we often forget how much it can encourage a young lawyer. Praise your supervisees when praise is deserved. It will encourage them to be the best lawyers they can be, which leads to my last tip: you must believe in the associate and in yourself as a supervisor. The human capacity for improvement is sometimes overestimated, but don't under-estimate it either. Care. If you don't have high expectations for your supervisee's improvement, you should not be his or her

supervisor.

Equally important, believe in your ability to help. It's not helpful to scrawl "wordy," or "awkward," or "disorganized" on a draft. Chances are the associate recognizes such symptoms of bad writing but needs help in finding a cure. Be specific about what's wrong and what it will take to make it right. If your partners aren't skilled at supervising, they can and should be trained. Often a partnership retreat is a good setting for a workshop on supervisory skills.

Finally be realistic and modest about what can be done in a given time period. A lawyer worthy of an equity share in your firm will not be created overnight. Look instead for progress and commitment. Take it from somebody who spends lots of time selling formal training programs: they can contribute perhaps 15 percent to a lawyer's development. Don't sneeze at that 15 percent because it could make the difference between failure and success, between profitability and marginality. Nevertheless, the rest is up to you as supervisor, coach, and on-the-job trainer. In the last analysis, excellent supervision is the principal means of developing associates into lawyers worthy of being your partners.

Guide the Way Down
Your Partnership Track

Whoever first called it "the partnership track" had a pretty good sense of metaphor. Working one's way through a law firm from entry level to equity ownership typically follows a certain track or course.

But there are tracks and tracks. A railroad track is precisely planned, carefully built, and fixed firmly to the earth, all to ensure the train goes exactly where it should go. A track through the forest primeval, however, is likely to be improvised, obscure, hard to follow, and even dangerous. Think of those poor hobbits in Tolkien's *Lord of the Rings*. In most law firms, the partnership track more closely resembles the lost path through the forest of Mirkwood than the Japanese "Bullet Train."

Recently a third-year associate with a moderate-sized firm said to me, "I like my job. I like the firm. But I don't know where I am or how I'm doing. I'm supposed to be specializing in real estate law, but I have no idea whether I'm getting the kind of work I need to make partner here." I often hear similar laments. Within your own firm, you probably hear them too or have them reported to you.

It's easy to dismiss the complaints of young lawyers as immaturity — the inability to live with the ambiguities and pressures of real world practice. But that's not fair and, from your point of view, it's not good business. The young lawyer quoted above is actively working with headhunters to find a new job in a firm similar to the one in which he feels adrift. And his departure will represent a substantial capital loss for the firm just as he is approaching real profitability. So there are solid business reasons for doing what you can to make the partner-ship track more like a railroad and less like an unpredictable adventure out of a Tolkien novel. And there are practical steps you can take towards that goal.

First, prepare a list of operational tasks associates should master. You may have already identified the legal skills neces-sary to qualify for partnership. They likely include a knowledge and understanding of the law and how it works; the capacity to marshal and order facts conceptually; the ability to write clearly and persuasively; the ability to make an effective oral argu-ment; the ability to interview, counsel, and instill confidence in clients; the ability to negotiate; and the ability to get along with other lawyers in the firm and elsewhere. If you have codified your own set of characteristics, you probably also evaluate your associates against them. If you don't, you should.

These general skills are required more or less by all lawyers, no matter their specialties. But your young lawyers also need guidance about operational tasks. What should a real estate lawyer in your firm be able to do after her first year? After her third year? Fifth? What should a member of your litigation de-partment have accomplished before he makes partner? When should a lawyer take the lead in preparing her first 10-K?

Just as an example, let's focus on some of the guideposts you might want to set out for your new real estate lawyers. They will want to know when and how you expect them to prepare sub-division documents, declarations of covenants, condominium agreements, commercial leases, property management docu-ments; to handle or assist in zoning matters, residential real estate closings, and commercial real estate negotiations; to deal with environmental agencies; to handle workouts for clients facing their own or another party's financial embarrassment; and so on.

You should inventory the operational tasks that lawyers in each specialty department must master. Of course a checklist won't eliminate the need to consider every lawyer individually. Nor will these career profiles or task lists represent the final word on what it is to be a specialist: you will probably revise them constantly, and your partners will forever debate the ap-propriate developmental stage for each prescribed task. Moreover, every associate won't reach these guideposts at the same moment in his or her career. When work has to be done, you must assign it whether or not it meets your pedagogical ideals. Sometimes one of the matters you want to assign for training purposes doesn't appear for years on end, and when it does appear it is too big, complex, or urgent to be used effec-tively in your training program.

Set up your task lists anyhow. The discipline of deciding what in fact you want your lawyers to be able to do will be enormously valuable for your firm's long-range business planning, as well as your recruiting and training programs. For the first time, you may have a pretty clear idea of the kind of lawyers you want to hire and the kind of partners you want to develop.

Lawyers often defer developing task lists on the pretext that they're not practical. But they're as practical as any checklist or form, not perfect, but enormously useful — indeed essential to systematic law practice. We avoid formulating task lists because it's not an easy undertaking: it requires time and imagination. But the job can be done. You will find that task lists will establish standards and goals to try for.

Some say task lists are just another ritual contrived to coddle young lawyers. In fact, the opposite is true: young lawyers can take responsibility for their own development if they know what you want. Task lists will give them better clues than they probably have presently.

Moreover, task lists can clarify your expectations. Most firms will encounter the associate who professes utter disbelief upon being told that he or she is not likely to make partner. But if you develop and adhere to a system of specialty task lists, you'll have a much easier time explaining to floundering associates why they are failing, how they can improve or — ultimately — why they should begin packing up and preparing resumes.

The partnership track can be straight, narrow and true, or serpentine and aimless. Perhaps in most firms it closely resembles the course for a road race. In that case, bear in mind that a road map can't win the Grand Prix — but it would be impossible to compete without one.

Assigning Work Is the Most Creative Aspect of Supervising Associates

In early 1984, the National Association for Law Placement reported that in the first year, a new associate costs approximately $100,000 to recruit and keep. Figure on laying out another $150,000 before you can honestly count the associate as a profit center. Even if your firm somehow gets by for less, it's clear that associate productivity is an ever more important factor in law office management. And your associates will derive most of their productivity gains from the on-the-job training they receive, whether or not you have a formal in-house program. The key to good on-the-job training is how work is assigned.

Law firms use several different methods for assigning work. The traditional one rotates new associates through several departments. But the rotation system has fallen on hard times because it is extraordinarily inefficient. Rotation made sense when associates worked for a few thousand dollars a year: The overhead needed to support them was negligible, small cases were available for training purposes, and clients were far more docile about paying for associate on-the-job training. Modern practice has largely eliminated these luxuries, however.

Even in the good old days, rotation had its drawbacks. Partners were loathe to make meaningful work assignments to inexperienced lawyers who were only passing through their departments. Given the choice of spending time with an associate who has chosen your specialty and one who will be gone and forgotten in a few weeks or months, all but the most altruistic partners will choose the former.

Moreover, associates as well as partners have become frus- **135** trated with the rotation system. Driven to succeed — and to do so as quickly as possible — associates generally resent the rotation system, which compels them to spin their wheels for a year or more when they could be establishing themselves in their careers within a chosen department.

Some firms acknowledge that rotation is inefficient and frustrating, but insist the costs are outweighed by the benefits: a law firm of lawyers who understand more than a narrow legal specialty and have worked with a cross-section of the firm's partners. Like many attractive vestiges of legal practice from the golden era, however, rotation is gradually losing out to economic reality.

Some firms have substituted a pooling system, a less-than-complete retreat from the notion that young lawyers should receive a basic grounding in all aspects of legal practice. Under pooling, one or more partners oversee a work assignment system that is supposed to accomplish two objectives: to get the clients' work done, and to give young lawyers a variety of assignments.

But the pooling system suffers from the same economic drawbacks as rotation. To the extent that assigning partners achieve the first objective — getting the work out — associates often fail to gain the second, a liberal education. And there's the pervasive problem of kidnapping. The system is in constant danger of breaking down when partners kidnap associates and make assignments to them in the corridors.

Thus more and more law firms are immediately assigning new associates to specialty departments. This expedient system satisfies associates because they know they are launched on the partnership track (barring mistakes in assignments, which can be rectified). And partners are more likely to devote themselves to training novices who will stick around and repay the time invested.

Frankly, each of these three systems for assigning work can produce creditable results. In fact the system used is not nearly as important as the way in which each specific piece of work is assigned. The following tips, if taken seriously, will dramatically improve on-the-job training and lawyer productivity in your firm, no matter whether you rotate, pool, fold, mutilate, or spindle associates.

First, resist the paths of least resistance. Lawyers generally fall victim to two. The first is the "I can do it better myself" path. Of course, senior lawyers can do almost any given legal task better than a tyro, but they also can and should do other, more important things that the tyro can't. How often do your partners draft written interrogatories, motions, contracts, and briefs, when they should be establishing strategy and tactics, reinforcing client relations, managing the firm, or rainmaking? We practice together in law firms to ensure that the work is performed efficiently. Yet too many of us continue to act like independent feudal barons, with only tenuous relations with one another and little faith in delegating work. Work is efficiently performed when it is assigned to the lowest possible level at which it will be done well. Thus the quality of your firm's work is not a function of who does it but who supervises it. A good manager (unlike a feudal baron) knows how to delegate and how to supervise work. A poor manager tries to do it all himself.

The second path of least resistance is to regularly make assignments to subordinates who know how to do the work. On the face of it you'd think it was efficient to channel work to those who can most easily get it done. But if you constantly give assignments to the trusted aide who can carry them out with no supervision you will unfairly limit that aide's development, and you will fail to train the next generation. Law firms that suffer from this syndrome discover fifth-year associates doing second-year work, a highly unproductive situation.

Not only is that path of least resistance unproductive, it is also stultifying for your associates. These days associates who feel stultified phone headhunters and soon bid you farewell, long before you can recoup your investment in their recruitment and training.

Second, establish the parameters of the assignment. Lawyers love to complain that associates give them 50-page memos when the assignment calls for no more than five. Or they complain that they could have done the job in three hours and it took their associates 30. But did anybody *tell* the associate how long the job should take or how many pages the assignment should be?

New lawyers arriving from law school are accustomed to the rhythms of a semester, or a year, or three years. But you have clients with immediate needs that must be met quickly. Law students are graded on how many issues they can spot and cram into a blue book. You're not concerned with issue spotting, however, but with solving problems. Law students see the ideal manuscript as an intellectual rumination worthy of the *Harvard Law Review*. But you want the question framed succinctly, followed by the associate's proposed answer, with supporting analysis attached.

In other words, unless you tell young lawyers how much time or attention a job is worth, they will be in the dark. Sure, you may be wrong in your estimate. Encourage them to come back to you if they think you have put them on too tight a leash: debating these issues will teach them a great deal. And incidentally, you also may learn from the exercise if your initial judgment was wrong.

Third, be specific in assigning the work. If you are inclined to **137** make abstract assignments like "Find the product liability law of the state of Kentucky," the work you get back is likely to be unfocused and less useful. Associates are desperate to know the context in which they are working. And their productivity will increase if they feel they are part of the team. So, make assignments as specific as possible. Urge associates to look at the file and get a feel for the overall matter. Among other positive results of putting associates into the picture, they will be far more likely to exercise good judgment.

Fourth, don't make emergency assignments when no real emergency exists. Nothing is more demoralizing than to be burdened with an all-night rush job when the finished product sits on the partner's desk, unread and unused, for a week or two thereafter. If your work assignment system isn't operating properly, regardless of how systematized it is, partners will kidnap associates to get their work done. And if necessary, they will lie about the degree of urgency. You must reform your system if it is creating spurious emergencies that only demoralize your associates.

Fifth, help associates find the necessary research aids. Some lawyers think that associates develop true grit by reinventing the wheel every time they're given an assignment. Nonsense. Plenty of initiative and creativity can be exercised on the cutting edge of the work, but help them get to the cutting edge by suggesting where the best research materials, forms, checklists, and the like can be found. Chances are some of them are stashed behind your file cabinet, but unearthing them should not be part of your associates' learning experience.

We complain — and so do clients — when new lawyers take too long and even then don't do a comprehensive job. But they are, after all, *new*. How can they know where to locate highly specialized materials? You are the expert. And they can become experts faster if you don't play games, compelling them to search *de novo* for the Holy Grail when you found it three years ago.

Sixth, encourage associates to submit outlines and drafts. A few minutes invested with a young lawyer at the formulative stage of a project can keep the project on course. And yet too many busy partners don't make themselves available until many hours and several drafts have been wasted.

On the other hand, there are outlines and there are outlines. An old-fashioned topic outline is useless if it merely indicates that an Introduction will be followed by Recommendations and then the Discussion. Ask for a substantive outline that reveals the basic point of the document and then tracks the topics and subpoints throughout. The associate should make clear the reason for writing the document. If he or she isn't able to come up with the point, it's too soon to start writing anything down.

Perhaps you didn't explain the assignment clearly enough.

Seventh, bombard supervisees with paper. I hear associates throughout the country complain that they don't know what happens to their work product. Yet it takes no time to send copies of all documents on a matter to the associate working with you. Even if you don't have time to give feedback, the associate can follow what is happening to his or her drafts by seeing how much editing you do before sending the documents on.

Finally, don't punish associates with writing assignments. As children we may have been compelled to write on the blackboard 500 times: "I will not dip Mary's pigtail in the inkwell any more." As lawyers we are constantly punished by having to read so much terrible legal writing. We tend to associate writing with punishment.

Eliminate unnecessary legal writing. If you make an assignment that does not truly require a written memorandum, don't demand one. If instead you need a case or two, or a preliminary sense of what the law might be, urge your associate to devote time to the intellectual process rather than to translating the work into an unnecessary essay.

Supervising the work of younger lawyers is one of the most important and least examined responsibilities of legal practice. And the first step in the process of supervision is the work assignment: if you blow that, you can never recoup the loss, no matter how good a trainer you may be. If you blow making an assignment, your client will suffer, your associate will languish, and, ultimately, your pocketbook will cry out.

Offer Young Lawyers a Mentor, Even If Some Refuse the Offer

Think back to your early years in practice. Did you have a mentor? Did he strongly influence your career, your life? Some of you, I surmise, recall mentors who had enormous impact — for better or worse. Others are (in this sense, at least) self-made men or women. Still others (more than you might think) won't know because they don't have a very good idea of what a mentor is. Their thinking gets all fuzzy when supervision and mentoring are brought up — and they may not recognize the difference between the two. I have discussed supervision in past chapters, but this one is about mentoring — an important, but very different activity.

In Homer's *Odyssey*, Mentor is Ulysses' trusted friend. In Ulysses' absence, Mentor nurtures, protects, and educates Ulysses' son, Telemachus, introducing him to other leaders and guiding him to assume his rightful place in society. Mentor does not teach Telemachus specific skills: instead he nurtures personal, "professional," and civic development. He also helps Telemachus find his way in the hierarchy. Mentor socializes Telemachus in the ways and expectations of the community. In plain language, a mentor teaches a protege how to behave.

A mentor is a bit of a parent and an older peer, whose efforts and special concern push the protege toward realizing his full potential. In *The Seasons of a Man's Life*, Daniel Levinson describes the mentoring relationship as spontaneous, exclusive, long-lasting, and potentially so intense that when the protege "arrives," a complete breach often follows.

In a law firm a mentor can play many roles. He or she can **141** accelerate a protege's advancement; guide the protege through the social and political thickets of the law firm, the bar, and the world of grown-ups in general; introduce the protege to and advance his interests among key partners, clients, bar leaders, and community figures; offer advice, encouragement, counsel, and criticism; and serve as a personal and professional role model.

Some superstars don't need mentors. But many associates, even very talented ones, will never realize their full potential without them. Your firm can have the best formal training programs, a successful system for delegating work, excellent supervision, and terrific feedback and evaluation. Nevertheless, some of your potentially excellent young lawyers will wipe out without good mentoring. So your promising but unspectacular young lawyers certainly need a mentor system.

What does the mentor himself get out of it? Plenty. A mentor is rewarded with the satisfaction of having helped develop young professionals who will in turn sustain his ideals — and even perhaps help fund his retirement. He also gains the insights into his professional and personal life that might not have come without guiding someone else.

The firm benefits in several ways. Young lawyers nurtured by mentors may be committed enough to the firm to accept 80-hour work weeks and resist the blandishments of zealous headhunters. The self-assured protege of a good mentor will be a productive lawyer. And the firm that has developed a network of mentors and proteges will be more cohesive, inspire more cooperation, and generally be a happier place to work. Finally, alumni of a firm that provides good mentors will speak well of the place.

Good mentoring relationships thus are important and ought to be cultivated. But how? First, don't confuse mentors with supervisors. Supervisors delegate work, maintain quality control, give practical tips on how to get the work done, and critique it. Mentors orient, support, socialize, and advocate.

Don't confuse these roles if you can help it: encourage mentoring relationships to develop apart from day-to-day supervisory relationships. New lawyers should be offered formal mentoring when they first arrive. Ideally, mentors should be emotionally suited to the task and disposed to give it the time and energy it requires. They ought to come from another part of the firm, not so distant that mentor and protege can't occasionally talk shop, but not so close that the mentor is likely to assign work to the protege.

Some young lawyers will reject your choice of a mentor for them and find their own. Splendid. Others will have no use for a mentor. That's OK, too. You should establish the formal mentoring system for those young lawyers who need mentors but are incapable of making the connection themselves. Is a formally assigned mentor as good as the one a young lawyer discovers himself in due course? Is an arranged marriage as good as a love marriage? The answer is: sometimes. The same holds true for assigned mentors. And some arranged marriages develop into very loving relationships.

This brings up the question of compatibility — as important between mentor and protege as between husband and wife. A purely arbitrary system of assigning mentors is thus unlikely to work. Some men, for example, cannot imagine being a mentor to a woman. Other men can imagine it all too well. A recent study found that many senior men hesitate to mentor women because they fear rumors of sexual involvement. Others fear actual sexual involvement will result from the intimacy of mentoring. The mentoring relationship of William Agee, late of the Bendix Corporation, and Mary Cunningham is a case in point: they experienced both rumor and reality, allegedly in that order. Sexual innuendo can be minimized, however, if not eliminated by establishing a comprehensive mentoring program. Rumors can hardly thrive in a situation where mentoring relationships are the rule rather than the exception.

Many firms rail desperately against formal mentoring systems, claiming that their partners are already burdened with management and administration on top of their practice. But mentoring is more a matter of quality time than endless time. A good mentor can even be responsible for three or four proteges at once: one may require an hour or two a week, another may require none, and the others will need attention only on an occasional basis.

Not everyone needs a mentor for success, nor is mentoring a panacea for professional incompetence or the occasional serious psychological problem. But good mentors have made an enormous difference in the professional lives of many lawyers. And any firm that wants to get the most out of its hiring and training will also match up needy proteges with all the mentors it can muster.

Nothing Means More for Lawyer Development Than Positive Feedback

Scared. I'm always scared. I think this is the one where I get found out.

Many of us have had a chance to gape at those folks in Las Vegas and Atlantic City who spend their days feeding money into slot machines. On occasion, some of us have even been those folks.

Why do they do it? Don't they know that the house unmercifully rigs the odds in its own favor? They do it because they are demonstrating the theory of intermittent reward: the odds may be terrible, but now and then the house pays off.

We're all the same. Like gambling fanatics, we can be induced to spend 2,400 billable hours a year in the service of a law firm, but only if the house pays off once in a while. Part of the payoff is expected to be cash. But every relevant study in the field of management psychology has shown that money isn't enough: the house has to pay off with psychic rewards, too. We call it positive feedback.

The theory of intermittent reward is not the only justification for positive feedback, however. Your young lawyers are superachievers. They come to you from decades of regular positive reinforcement in the form of grades, acceptance at elite schools, academic honors, and lots of psychological support. When they enter legal practice they are often cast adrift for the first time, likely to hear from their supervisors only when they screw up.

Moreover, many high achievers think that they're phonies. "Buried in the hearts of many high achievers is the secret sense of being a fraud, and the constant fear of being exposed," wrote Daniel Goleman in the *New York Times*. In fact, the conviction that one is a phony may occur in as many as two out of every **145** five successful people, according to one researcher. Other studies show that 70 percent of the population have felt themselves to be impostors for at least some period of their lives. Such feelings may be intensified when an entry-level lawyer moves into a new position at a competitive law firm.

Thus, a large portion of your young lawyers may be convinced that they are the flukes who slipped through the recruiting net. When busy partners fail to give them positive feedback, your new lawyers are psychologically incapable of interpreting the silence as satisfaction with their performance. Instead, they read silence as deliberate coldness, a sign of displeasure — as evidence to support the lurking suspicion that they are impostors.

The results can be devastating. Some very competent lawyers will decide to bail out at the first opportunity, certain (though wrong) that shortly they will be pushed out. And those lawyers who do stick around, despite the lack of positive feedback, will likely be operating at less than peak performance. They may be distracted by fear of the unknown ("Am I making it here?"), or convinced that extra effort yields no discernible results.

If I were a headhunter, the first thing I'd ask my intended targets would be: "When was the last time you heard positive feedback? Something more detailed than a hurried 'good job.'" This tactic would, I think, quickly yield me more heads than I could barter if I could promise them more positive feedback in their new jobs.

Yet the reasons for not giving positive feedback are not at all apparent. Positive feedback is cheap and relatively simple. It takes little time to prepare and deliver. Hardly any senior lawyers are so curmudgeonly as to be incapable of saying nice things, at least once in a while. And we don't (or shouldn't) have young lawyers around who never deserve praise.

But unfortunately, despite the importance of positive feedback and the relatively low cost of providing it, we don't do it. Here's what associates in an assortment of firms across the country have told me: "Looking back on my first reviews, I was just a paranoid little kid. I have never perceived what reviews meant." One said, "Partners frequently treat associates with near disdain, making themselves unapproachable." Partners at that firm probably didn't think they were treating him and his peers with "near disdain," but lack of positive feedback is perceived as a sign of disdain. At another firm I heard, "The feedback, if there is any, tends to be negative." And: "We only get feedback when we screw up — if then."

We know that supervising young lawyers and delivering negative feedback are skills that must be learned, and that they take some time and attention. But providing positive feedback is simple. All that's required is sensitivity, thoughtfulness, and a little time to explain in detail to your young lawyer why you liked the job he or she did, how it made your life easier and the client happier. When positive feedback is delivered with care, young lawyers respond with improved levels of performance. Praise will not only communicate your high expectations of them but — at the same time — will elevate their own belief in what they can accomplish.

The quotation at the beginning of this chapter is from Tom Stoppard's play, *The Real Thing*. Annie, an accomplished and successful actress, is rehearsing for her next starring role. She has every reason to be confident, but she's not: *"I think this is the one where I get found out."* Annie will be good, and she will know she's good because the audience will applaud and the critics will praise her. In a law firm, you are audience and critic. Don't risk losing some of your best young lawyers because you can't take the time to applaud.

Communicate with Your Associates — If You Want to Keep Them

President Jimmy Carter got himself into trouble when he went on television to announce that the nation suffered from a "malaise." Nevertheless, I have to report that we are discovering a malaise in law firms. Whether they have 13 or 300 lawyers, we find that more and more of their associates feel that they are exploited, distrusted, untrained, and unwanted. As a result, they leave well before their employers want them to — before their firms have recouped the investment in recruitment and training. Furthermore, those who stay may not produce their best work, and their productivity may not be up to its potential either. At the least, this malaise makes the law firm less than the happiest place to spend 10 to 14 hours a day.

Oddly, these dissatisfied associates seem to gripe hardly at all about being overworked and underpaid. Indeed, associates in competitive firms are more or less overpaid, at least in relation to the salaries of a generation ago. Of course times have changed, law school tuition has shot up, and many young lawyers need their salaries to pay off education loans as well as their rents. But so long as law firms don't fall too far behind the going rate (which is the rate you have to pay to keep them from going), salary is an issue that remains in the background.

The quantity of work, though important, seems also to be less of an issue than before. Of course actual workloads vary enormously. I have consulted with firms in which associates bill an average of 1,450 hours, and others in which the average is 2,100 hours and up. The strange thing is that the malaise is as widespread among 1,450-hour lawyers as it is among the workaholics.

Nor does the problem seem to be geographical. Some of the most disaffected associates are with relatively small firms in middle-sized cities, in the Sun Belt as well as the Rust Belt.

We needn't speculate about the possible consequences of this malaise. They are already with us, and they are severe. Partners in several firms have phoned me recently, stunned by the unexpected departure of one or more superstar associates who knew or should have known that they were right on the partnership track. Overall turnover rates seem to be edging up while morale and productivity are on the way down. These statistics confirm our findings in confidential interviews with associates. Almost invariably we ask them if they want to be partners in their firms, and very few say yes. Perhaps some are defending against disappointment; others may be unwilling to display ambition before a stranger.

But I think that a growing number are seriously disaffected by the idea of practicing law in the current atmosphere. They describe it as a "We-They" environment, one in which partners pay almost exclusive attention to clients and compensation and ignore associates. Partners, associates say, focus only on associates' mistakes — and only in a uselessly critical way. And this is not what most associates bargained for, unless they hired on with one of the relatively few Wall Street-type firms that never made a pretense of giving recruits a good crack at partnership. (Some of those firms, incidentally, are falling far short of their hiring quotas.)

"But," you might say, "it's not really like that. We are very concerned about associates and spend a hell of a lot of time and money not directed at short-term profit." I'm sure that's true. However, it's not the facts but associates' perceptions that are causing the malaise. If you sense that your firm is not immune to it, how can you cure this disaffection? First, if we can determine the cause, it might suggest its own cure.

Every firm with the problem tends to have grown significantly. Some have grown to a truly gargantuan size, with many widely scattered offices. Others have grown from six to 13 lawyers. But the results are the same. The old loyalty and collegiality have disappeared, perhaps partly because of increased size or geographical scattering, but also because of the quickened, some might say frenzied, pace of modern practice. The common denominator in these firms is a communications breakdown.

Everybody likes to talk about the olden days, but there is no way now to restore the characteristics natural to a smaller organization in a different era. In fact I'm a little skeptical that the good old days were so great. Be that as it may, no magic solution can restore what used to be a natural closeness between small numbers of associates mostly on the partnership track and partners who were also comparatively at ease. The communication between associates and partners that might once have happened naturally must instead be restored through systematic procedures.

For instance, you need a system of assigning work that ensures a feedback loop. Associates must have access to partners if and when the system breaks down; that is, when they are receiving too much or too little work. Even more important, associates must feel that assignments are made not only to move the firm's work out the door, but also to develop their professional skills so that they will either make partner or be marketable elsewhere.

Furthermore, assignments must fully inform the associate. Nothing is more likely to reinforce the We-They syndrome than simply dumping a file on an associate's desk, or ordering him to answer a purely abstract research question. It's hard to feel like a professional if work comes to you in much the same way it does to an assembly line worker.

Associates must also have access to the partner in charge. Lawyers seem almost totally blind to the need for adequately supervising the work they delegate. Corporate managers, on the other hand, tend to delegate almost everything. They are paid to supervise. But for most lawyers, supervision is a misunderstood and unappreciated aspect of their professional lives. Without the training and incentive to supervise, they are as likely as not to leave associates to their own devices until the work is completed. At that point, the senior lawyer either does it over himself or looses a barrage of useless invective against the confused associate. It's not enough to say "My door is always open. Come see me if you have a question." Part of being a good supervisor is helping young lawyers understand what the essential questions are. Law firms could save enormous amounts of time if their partners efficiently supervise work in progress.

In the last chapter I harangued you about the importance of positive as well as negative feedback. To feel good about training and development, an associate must get the feedback that will help improve his performance and at the same time increase self-confidence.

Of course, some firms consider their periodic performance assessments a substitute. However, if these reviews are conducted by lawyers who constitute the polite equivalent of a Mafia hit squad, they'll do little good. Periodic performance assessment can be an important tool for evaluating young lawyers, determining their relative economic value to the firm, and comparing their progress to their peers'. But this process does almost nothing to stimulate their development, reinforce their professional strengths, and eliminate their weaknesses. **151**

You can much more effectively show associates that you care about them through regular and immediate feedback and through remedial programs designed to help them succeed.

And some young lawyers need mentors, but cannot develop such relationships on their own, so the firm must assign mentors, however artificial that may seem. Sometimes those artificial assignments may not work. But even if they work only occasionally, they will help dispel the aura of estrangement and distrust.

Here's another important kind of communication: lateral hires should not be a surprise to associates. Labor lawyers demand that their corporate clients post job descriptions and encourage internal applications. In a law firm, such a formal process may seem pretentious, but associates still need to be informed of — and should help define — the firm's professional needs. Associates can also be a good source of leads for lateral hires. But here, as elsewhere, they will be far more content with the process if they are made part of it.

You should also inform associates of management issues. Why should the firm withhold regular data (except perhaps about compensation paid to individual lawyers) from mid-level and senior associates? Tradition only. Or possibly the fear of being written up in the *American Lawyer*.

But disaffected associates will leak facts — or fiction — to the *American Lawyer* anyhow. So what harm can disclosing the facts do? Moveover, annual studies such as those performed by Peat, Marwick, & Mitchell Co. go a long way toward letting it all hang out.

Associates kept in the dark about writeoffs, accounts receivable, business plans, and the like will always imagine the situation to be worse, and the partners more avaricious, than they are. But associates regularly informed of management issues will be better equipped to grapple with them when, and perhaps even before, they themselves become partners. We know that excluding associates estranges them: are the benefits of excluding them worth the cost?

Finally, training programs can bring lawyers closer. Of course they will yield better quality work and improve productivity. But they can also pay big dividends by improving the flow of communications. Lawyers in a learning situation relate to each other in a way that bypasses the pressures and strains of the regular work day. Furthermore, your investment in a formal training program clearly signals associates that you care about their development as well as their output.

There are healthy arguments against my recommended cure for the malaise of modern law firms. And certainly no firm is likely to fill the entire prescription. But show me a firm that has taken none of these steps to include associates, and I will show you a firm with morale problems, high turnover, and serious difficulties bagging its annual quota of recruits. If your size is stable or shrinking, you won't much care. But if you want to grow or are growing, you'd better care plenty.

Letter to Associates I: Partners Don't Understand You

I have said in an earlier chapter that there is a communications gap between senior and junior lawyers. I even characterized the situation as a crisis — a "malaise." Yet we experts, or — to use a dirty word — consultants, spend our time consulting with senior partners, to the neglect of the junior lawyers who are our common concern. So this chapter is for associates — trainees rather than trainers. If you're a partner, share it with them. You may even want to schedule a meeting of associates and partners to discuss these issues.

Dear Associate,

You have chosen to try the world of corporate law. Whether you've been in it for five days or five years, you know that it's an intense and difficult world. I needn't tell you about the demands and stresses of the work — high standards, short deadlines, huge workloads, diminishing partnership opportunities. I want instead to share with you some thoughts from my own experience (a while ago) as a new lawyer in a large, corporate firm, and more recently from six years of thinking and writing about practice management and lawyer development.

In this first letter I'll examine how partners and associates view each other. In the next letter I'll suggest ways that young lawyers can get the most out of on-the-job training.

You probably feel that older partners don't understand you. Every generation lives in a different world from the one that went before. In the olden days, firms took on associates the same way the Church took on priests: the novice undertook an act of faith in the Church and its priesthood. Novices in the Church and associates in the law firm were expected to live in poverty, not just to enrich the Church or the firm but because worldly distractions would prevent full concentration on the work at hand. Previously, associates placed their faith in the firm and its partners. Whatever was needed, the young lawyer did; none ever questioned whether the demands were reasonable. Enough that they were made. For those associates who gave themselves fully to the firm — who were able to accept the faith — and do the work — the rewards were great.

But dramatic changes have occurred in the past generation. First, successful lawyers' dollar earnings have multiplied, but their wealth and status have diminished. In earlier times, corporate lawyers made big money when big money meant big houses, servants, high culture, and public respect. Today, corporate practice seems to be esteemed only in a handful of national law schools. And even though partners earn far more money than they used to, few senior lawyers have manor houses staffed with servants. Senior partnership no longer offers automatic membership in the power elite. In fact, far from being revered by businessmen, senior partners have to scramble to keep old clients and get new ones. Their friends in the corporate world no longer see lawyers as high priests or medicine men. Instead they expect them to bid competitively on legal services just as suppliers of other services do.

To make matters worse, many corporate law firms have grown exponentially in the past 20 years. Thus they are competing not only for business but also for the best and brightest law graduates to do the work. Today's senior partners were recruited when law firms were on top and the recruit made an act of faith. But your firm probably scrabbled with other top firms to woo you. The shoe is now on the other foot. Whereas once recruits had to make a law firm believe in them, today the act of faith has been reversed — a law firm has to convince its recruits that it will invest everything — care, feeding, training, and a lot of money — in its associates.

Senior partners tell me that they don't understand the new arrangement. After all, they bring in the business. Their clients perceive them as supreme in their specialties. Yet they must defer to the "whims" of you associates. They have to "coddle" you. I have oversimplified these feelings to make a point, but most senior lawyers share them to some degree. When I entered corporate practice 20 years ago, no sane person could have predicted that a national legal publication would annually evaluate summer clerkship programs, giving points for partying. Not even a loony would have imagined that lawyers and law students would take the damn thing seriously!

In other words, circumstances have led senior partners to be more than a little ambivalent about you. But circumstances alone have not changed. You, the current generation of young lawyers are palpably different from your predecessors. You aren't humble. You aren't poor. You question whether weekend appearances at the office are necessary when no work presses. You refuse to subordinate the rest of your life to the needs — real or imagined — of the firm. Chances are you don't have a traditional one-income family, with a spouse to manage base camp while you devote whatever it takes, and then some, to the partnership quest.

When it comes to your work, you prefer being brought in on the matter at the outset — being given the big picture. You don't see much benefit for your own training and development in carrying out a series of unrelated tasks where you can't see the forest for the trees. You want to be participants... one might almost say partners. And you don't like being treated as members of a group rather than discrete, nonconforming professionals. You are likely to be women or of different ethnic backgrounds from the majority of your mostly male senior partners.

What makes senior partners especially uneasy is their feeling that partners are partners, associates are associates, and associates should respect — indeed revere — the difference. Yet they also feel compelled to accommodate you, even if they don't understand you. And indeed they must accomodate you — because the profession has opened up, one might even say exploded. Very likely you could get on the elevator in your building, get off a half dozen floors up or down, and be hired by that law firm, which will be as desperate as your current firm for first-class talent.

Your problems with senior partners are no worse than those you face with younger ones. These men and women are going flat out to make it. They danced as fast as they could to make partner only to find that the dancing doesn't end with partnership but only just begins there. Unlike university tenure, law firm partnership is not a license to coast or to choose one's own direction and pace because increasingly a partner's income is decided by his or her production, or dollars received for work accomplished. So billable hours and minimal writeoffs are at a premium. Thus young partners have little time to nurture you; instead, they may harbor a short-sighted notion of efficiency and productivity that demands as little utilization of associates as possible.

They're wrong, of course. But their attitude derives from real problems in the development of lawyers. In law school, you are trained to think like a lawyer, but the training is process-oriented. The law is a seamless web, you learn. A law review note may take a year or longer to write and be hundreds of pages long. Conflicts of laws can't be mastered in less than several months. No issue can be addressed in less than a 55-minute class. The highest grade goes to the student who spots the most legal issues on the exam.

But the practice of law is not process-oriented; it is problem- or client-oriented. A client needs advice fast. A TRO must be filed. A deal must close before the bridge loan expires, or interest rates change, or the unfriendly takeover occurs. But training a new lawyer to respond in real time to real problems itself takes time. Wrong as these young partners may be, they often prefer doing it themselves to taking that time.

These young partners may also see that the firm's growth in business has slowed down or stopped. Even though they can anticipate earning far more than the old guard, it's all too clear that there will never be Edwardian luxury in their lives. They see that additional partnership shares — your partnership shares — are likely to attenuate theirs. Now that they have been piped into the partnership, they wonder whether they ought to pull up the gangplank behind them.

Some negative perceptions of associates are shared by old and new partners alike. All older lawyers, for example, think that associates can't write. You can't. But neither can they. Typically what they mean is that your stylistic idiosyncrasies are not the same as theirs. One of your biggest problems is how to accommodate as many sets of such idiosyncrasies as there are lawyers for whom you prepare drafts. But in fairness, they often say you can't write when what they mean is that you write too much, or you write the wrong thing. For example, they expect a four-page memorandum and you deliver a 40-page tract. In the four-page memo they expected a condensed statement of the question, a sharp analysis of the issue, and a clear conclusion or recommendation. Instead, your 40-page essay represents the history of your research. It spots all the issues — law school style — but never comes to terms with what they mean to the client.

Partners, young and old, also wonder how committed associates really are to the firm. This is a fair question. Many associates wonder the same thing. When I interview associates, many frankly admit to being uncertain whether they want to make partner: there are other and perhaps better opportunities at similar firms, in lucrative business situations, or in predictable, secure corporate legal departments. However understandable your ambivalence may be, however, when partners question the depth of your commitment, there are consequences. Training young lawyers takes time and effort. But oppressed by your confusion and uneasiness, some senior partners will misread your attitude as lack of ambition or drive. And if partners harbor suspicions about your staying power, they may not want to invest that time and effort even in the young lawyer showing signs of becoming the next Brandeis.

So much for the bad news. The good news is that there are several steps you can take to overcome the generation gap, the expectations gap, and the understanding gap. In the next letter — the good news.

Letter to Associates II: How to Help the Firm Help You Develop

The last letter to associates explained why partners, old and young, have serious problems understanding the new generation of lawyers entering corporate practice. After delivering the bad news, I promised to follow it with a letter containing good news for associates, with advice on how to get ahead despite the very real problems they face.

First, compensate for your bosses' weaknesses. Lawyers get to be partners or senior lawyers in corporations and government agencies by being good lawyers — and by sticking around. As they develop, they pride themselves on their lawyerly prowess. But the more seniority they have, the more they are likely to become responsible for nonlawyering jobs, such as management. And most lawyers who think about management at all pretend it has to do only with timekeeping, billing, collections, automation, and marketing. They are right as far as that goes, but most managers fail to see that one of their biggest jobs is managing you — their most important asset. That means they need to make you as productive as possible as fast as possible. And as you are ever so painfully aware, senior lawyers often correlate your productivity only with hours billed.

You and I know, however, that maximum productivity depends on a number of factors: the kind of work assigned, the thoroughness with which the assignment is explained, the accessibility of the lawyer assigning the work, and feedback immediately after you complete assignments. Doing these things well are matters of good management, but many partners don't understand their importance. Even those who appreciate their **161** importance may lack the skills to do them well. So, if you want to succeed, you must help them out.

You should go after the work you need for your development. Some firms have elaborate systems for delegating work, whether on a rotation, pooling, or teaming basis. However, none of these systems is a perpetual motion machine. Each is only as good as the people managing it. Few totally replace the traditional system of grabbing an associate on the run. Whatever the system, though, the squeaky wheel does in fact get the grease. If you are getting burned out from too much of the same work, or if you are stuck with jobs from a partner who gives you no guidance or support, make the problem known to your assigning partner, or associates committee chairman, or department chairman, or mentor, or somebody. I have interviewed lots of associates who didn't let on that they were getting the short end of the work assignment stick until they handed in their resignations. And firm management was very sorry not to have had the chance to intervene earlier.

But remember to approach the subject as a negotiator, not an adversary. Don't be shrill and inflexible. They own the firm, after all, not you. On the other hand, don't be afraid to ask for a change of assignments or even of specialties because you're afraid the firm will say no. If the firm says no to your first request, think of it as if the firm were an umpire you had to argue with. You may not expect him to change his call this time, but next time he'll be more interested in your point of view.

Furthermore, insist on a full explanation of whatever job you're given. Too many busy lawyers practice the "dump and run" technique of assigning work: "Here's a file and a short memorandum. I need the job done by Tuesday." Of course, there are times when there's no other way to get the work out on time. Except for bona fide emergencies, however, you can't be expected to do a thorough job, or learn by doing it, unless the lawyer assigning the work adequately explains it to you. Nor should you assume that what you passively are told is all you need to know. Be feisty. Ask questions. Sometimes the answers to your questions — or lack thereof — will suggest that your boss isn't sure what's involved and you'll end up thinking through the job together. If you handle this kind of situation tactfully, you will have a terrific learning experience as well as one helluva grateful boss. So there are no stupid questions, only shy associates.

Some partners, however, are as elusive as the Loch Ness monster. This is despite the fact that I've never met a partner who didn't insist he was fully accessible to his juniors: "They know my door is always open," boast these paragons of collegiality. But they are always on the phone, in meetings, out of town, or just too important to bother. Well... bother anyway.

Find out when they are vulnerable — early in the morning, lunchtime, after five pm. Get in there while they're on the phone and wait them out.

When I started at a large corporate firm, I was afraid that nobody but me could be so stupid as to need guidance from time to time on work in progress. I now can admit that I was probably more stupid than most. But the truth is that the smartest of my peers and yours are the quickest to ask questions rather than waste time spinning their wheels. Your quandary may well be the result of a poor briefing when the job was assigned. Or it may arise out of a discovery you made that your boss did not anticipate.

Of course there's a difference between shaping your work by questioning and consulting with your boss, on the one hand, and on the other, asking your boss to do your job for you.

Also, since law firms are bigger than they used to be, you have another reason for dropping in frequently: partners remember the associate who makes an impression. And bouncing ideas off and seeking guidance from partners are better ways of making an impression than doing cartwheels down the firm's corridors.

Another good idea is to solicit immediate feedback. All human beings are reluctant to criticize one another (unless they're married to each other). Lawyers are more reluctant than most, perhaps because we believe professional independence demands that we be left free to make our own mistakes. Perhaps, but I rather think that reluctance to criticize junior lawyers comes from another source. The ability to give useful feedback — whether positive or negative — is just another management skill most lawyers never learn. But whatever the source, the lines of communication are definitely down. When we prepare firms for supervisory skills workshops, partners often say they are "too soft on associates" or that they "don't let young lawyers know where they're weak." Even more remarkable, associates have told us that they fail to seek feedback because they "don't want to embarrass the partner in charge."

Sure, partners have to learn to be more forthcoming. But so do you — don't wait around for the milennium. Overcome your reluctance to hear your work criticized and your exquisite sensibilities over the boss's feelings. You can't develop as a lawyer if you're in the dark about your progress. So demand feedback, but try to be sympathetic to the partner's own obligations and distractions. Ask that your meetings be scheduled regularly, at a time and place where you both can focus on the matter at hand.

When you do manage to get some feedback, listen actively to what you hear. Active listening sounds easier than it turns out to be. Instead of putting all your energy into excuses and defenses, **163** try rephrasing the points made criticizing your work to make sure that you've understood them correctly. It simply makes no sense to demand feedback and then shut yourself down psychologically when you get it.

As you probably already know, semiannual or annual reviews are too little, too late. And too often the criticism you get at that stage is anonymous and not very specific — which is to say, almost entirely useless to your development as a lawyer. Mayor Koch, whatever you may think of his politics, has built a pretty successful career by going around the boroughs of New York asking constituents, "How'm I doin'?" Being New Yorkers, they tell him. The same approach may help your legal career by getting you equally forthright responses.

One thing that may be especially difficult for you is to ask to be taken along. Yet observation is an irreplaceable way to learn how to practice law. And being an associate in a large firm gives you, theoretically, the opportunity to observe excellent lawyers in action. But today economic pressures discourage partners from inviting you along to observe, or even to perform from the second chair. To some extent, these economic pressures are the result of associates' salaries. But whatever the overhead burden, you still must be trained, and some observation and second chairing are essential.

Partners will vary considerably in their willingness to take you along or invite you in on a client interview or telephone conversation. Without being obnoxious or unreasonable, you can and should make known your interest in watching the proceedings.

You must also ask to see revisions of all your work. You can't improve your writing if you don't know what you're doing wrong. Yet many senior lawyers routinely revise or do over associates' work, and never share their revisions with the original draftsmen. Don't let that happen. At the outset of your relationship with a new boss, make it clear that you want the good and the bad news. Even when a senior lawyer doesn't have time to sit down and go over his revisions with you, he can surely send you photocopies. Read them. If they make sense, you will have been enlightened without any additional time costs to you or your boss. If you don't understand why he sullied your prose, go in and ask. You will either learn how to write better, or you will learn how to write worse to satisfy that particular lawyer.

Finally, it's a great tactic to pretend senior lawyers are your clients. And the best lawyers don't simply accept the client's perception of a problem: they dig for further facts and circumstances. They think creatively about previously unforeseen contingencies. They test their clients' basic assumptions and may recommend courses of action entirely different from those originally contemplated. Once a lawyer is on the job, he or she will regularly counsel the client about next steps, even prod the client, if necessary, to follow through.

It's now a cliche (though that makes it no less true) that busy professional women need wives. Well, busy lawyers need lawyers. If you want to dazzle your bosses, pretend they are your clients. Using your best bedside manner — as you would with real clients — examine the assignments they give you. Test their understanding of the problems. Suggest additional issues that should be explored. Don't just do the job as requested, but suggest what should be done next, or at least what should be considered next. You can even volunteer to take the next step yourself.

What better way could there be to learn how to satisfy clients than to practice on your senior partners? Moreover, nothing is as likely to win you favor in the hearts and minds of your bosses as an ability not only to do the job assigned, but also to take responsibility for work in process. Ultimately, when they vote on whether to take you into the partnership or not, think how nice it will be when several partners say that you are indispensable. Indeed, that you are *their* lawyer.

Teaching Practical Skills

Everybody Agrees That Legal Writing is Bad, and Here's What You Can Do About It

Legal writing is like television. Everybody thinks it's terrible but consensus explodes on the question of what to do about it. When Newton Minow was chairman of the Federal Communications Commission, he achieved instant fame by branding TV a "vast wasteland." Later, an enterprising reporter asked him how he would change things. He reportedly answered that he would like to see more Jimmy Durante on the tube. (Minow, now a senior partner in Chicago's Sidley & Austin, was — I am sure — misquoted. He serves as a trustee of the Chicago Symphony Orchestra and otherwise demonstrates very high aesthetic taste.)

Some would dismiss the issue of poor legal writing by arguing that nobody writes well anymore. Why should lawyers be held to a higher standard? The answer is obvious. The writing of lawyers is unique because people often must act according to their written instructions in contracts, opinion letters, and the like. Even more important, legal writing is constantly exposed to attack — by opposing counsel, by courts, and by frustrated clients. Doctors can get away with an insufferable writing style because they are judged on whether the patient recovers. Lawyers, on the other hand, are to a very large extent judged on what they write.

Lawyers all agree on the objectives of good legal writing. It should be clear, concise, persuasive, and precise. But they don't agree on what it takes to reach these objectives.

THE PROBLEMS

Here are some of the reasons offered for the poor state of legal writing:

- Lawyers write too much and organize their writing poorly.
- Their writing is imprecise, abstract, impersonal, and passive. It fails to persuade the reader.
- Too many sentences begin with prepositions and are riddled with prepositional phrases.
- Too many lawyers are ignorant of punctuation.
- They use archaisms, including "wherefore" and "whereas," and formalisms like "Now comes the plaintiff."
- They couple synonyms like "goods and chattels," "have and hold," "authorize and empower."
- They are addicted to unnecessary Latin phrases.
- They use insipid legal constructions like "said property" and "party of the first part."
- Their memos and briefs contain too many footnotes and are often a confusing maze of double and triple negatives.

Unfortunately, some of these characterizations are superficial. Improve punctuation so that every comma is a bull's-eye, eliminate all the old-fashioned words and constructions, and lawyers will not solve the fundamental problems of legal writing any more than fertilizing the TV channels with daily doses of Jimmy Durante would have caused that vast wasteland to bloom. Some of the other characterizations of bad legal writing are accurate and profound, but recognizing them does not necessarily help solve the problems. For example, telling a lawyer that his writing is wordy, or unpersuasive, or impersonal is like telling the victim of a terrible accident that he is injured. The challenge is to save his life.

Several law school professors and a small army of journalists have made careers of spotlighting awkward and embarrassing characteristics of incompetent legal writing. In their books and lectures, they mainly state the obvious — "verbal tics are bad" — and preach the gospel — "write clearly, concisely, and precisely." They mean well, but so does the speech coach who merely admonishes his pupil not to stutter.

RECOGNIZING BAD WRITING

In Government Documents

In 1984, United States District Judge Jack B. Weinstein struck a blow for justice and literacy when he held that bad writing in government documents violated due process rights protected by the Constitution. Weinstein ordered the Department of Health and Human Services (HHS) to clean up its review letters to Medicare claimants, finding that they "are not only incomprehensible," but also contain "insufficient and misleading" information. The judge characterized HHS's language as "gobbledegook, jargon . . . and doublespeak. It does not qualify as English." Medicare patients disputing amounts reimbursed are entitled to "comprehensible explanations of the actual reason full reimbursement is denied." (*David v. Heckler*, Civ. Action No. 79 C 2813, E.D.N.Y. July 11, 1984).

Judge Weinstein's remedy is by his own admission less than detailed, but it seems to include an order to HHS lawyers to cooperate with plaintiffs' lawyers in arranging voluntary changes in Medicare prose and procedures. If this holding stands, Judge Weinstein will be remembered forever as the man who formulated the constitutional right to clear writing. That's enough honor, heaven knows, for any man. But it remains for even more clever Solons to craft an adequate remedy. Who can help but be amused by Judge Weinstein's notion that *lawyers* — of all people — are somehow able to clarify the convoluted and confusing correspondence of bureaucrats.

One of the letters at issue in *David v. Heckler* contained the following sentence: "The amounts are based on statistics covering customary charges on an individual physician and prevailing rates by all physicians rendering similar services in a given locality." Nobody's going to imagine that Abraham Lincoln or E.B. White crafted that sentence, but it doesn't strike me as violating the Due Process Clause, either. It's not, I think, any worse than this one: "Doubt as to whether this type of claim should be construed as barred by section 205(h), 42 U.S.C. 405(h), should be resolved in favor of finding jurisdiction since the availability of judicial review for constitutional questions is generally 'presumed.'"

This sentence, is, of course, from Judge Weinstein's opinion. Forget his confusing use of "since" (which denotes the passage of time) instead of "because." The sentence seems long and confusing because the reader is not told who's doing what to whom. Judge Weinstein could have done his readers a great service merely by using action verbs and agents of the action in the subject position of the sentence. "Courts generally 'presume' that judicial review is available for constitutional questions. Therefore, we should not construe section 205(h), 42 U.S.C. 405(h) to bar jurisdiction of this type of claim."

Look how many virtuous changes can be wrought. The rewrite contains two shorter sentences instead of one breathlessly long one. The original had 35 words. The two sentences of the rewrite together contain only 25 words. Think how lawyers' lives and the lives of their clients would improve if all legal writing were condensed by almost one-third. The passage now presents two ideas in concrete terms (courts presume; therefore we   **171** should not construe the law to bar). These ideas are now persuasively sequenced, with the "old" or orienting idea (courts presume) preceding the important conclusion (we shouldn't construe the law to bar jurisdiction).

The point is not to denigrate an important decision by one of the nation's best jurists, but to suggest that the lousy writing problem is as unlikely to be solved by lawyers as the ethics in government problem is by ABSCAM politicians.

By Law Professors

Lawyers even at the source of the mother tongue can't generally be understood. I was amused as well as confused by an article I discovered one summer in London. Professor R.M. Goode is pitching a CLE course, Principles of Legal Drafting, held at Cambridge University: "We might therefore reasonably assume that our legislation and legal documents would reflect not merely an intention to produce a particular legal effect but also a need to communicate that effect to readers of normal intelligence by the use of language they would understand." Perhaps the good Professor Goode means that people should be able to understand what public and private lawmakers write, but I can't understand what he has written.

Meanwhile, the American Bar Association (ABA) reinforces the skepticism in the legal profession's ability to write the right stuff. When the Supreme Court came down with its decision in *Hishon v. King & Spaulding*, ABA president Wallace D. Riley issued a statement that contained this expression of policy: "The full participation and contribution of women lawyers in the profession is a goal from which the ABA and American society will benefit." If this isn't gobbledegook, what is? Translated into English, the ABA is not asserting that "If women fully participate in and contribute to the profession of law, the ABA and American society will benefit." That is bland enough, but there's less there than meets the eye. Parsed correctly, the statement says that the ABA and American society will benefit from the goal of full participation and contribution of women lawyers in the profession. What? You say that's virtually meaningless? In its original form, it didn't seem quite so empty, did it?

Could Wally Riley be a crafty male chauvinist pig? He could be; but with a brilliant, charming, and stylish wife who has been a judge among other things, I don't think so. Which means that he didn't intend to say something as silly as his official statement.

Okay. It's easy to pick on the ABA. So here's an excerpt from Harvard University's Statement of Rights and Responsibilities: "Interference with members of the University in performance of their normal duties and activities must be regarded as unacceptable obstruction of the essential proceses of the University."

With a law professor as president and a school full of law professors eager to draft a legal code for every new volcanic atoll that emerges from the Pacific Ocean, Harvard can't come up with a comprehensible set of rules for itself. The excerpt violates almost every principle of clear writing. It takes a bunch of perfectly decent verbs and freezes them into nouns (interfere, perform, obstruct). It doesn't explain what happens when A does something to B. As a result, the reader is left with no guidance at all as to what one can or cannot do, and no idea of the consequences. No wonder Law School Dean James Vorenberg had no luck when he tried to use the statement to exorcise students from faculty meetings.

Vorenberg probably drafted it; it reads more than a little like a Vorenberg article in last year's *Harvard Law Record*:

> Expressions of disapproval, such as those made when a speaker is introduced or made briefly in response to particular statements, are themselves exercises of listeners' rights to make their views known. While it is difficult to define precisely the permissible range of such expressions, repeated and prolonged shouting or other conduct that interferes with the ability to hear a speaker's statements violates the rights of both the speaker and the audience as a whole.

Sometimes the purpose *is* to obscure. Harvard Law School and its ilk train lawyers remarkably well to write obscurely. But surely, when drafting statutes, rules, or guidelines they should write clearly and precisely. Vorenberg might have said something like this:

> Any of us may express disapproval when a speaker is introduced or says something controversial. That's our right. But that right must give way to the speaker's right to be heard and his audience's right to listen. I don't know exactly where one set of rights must yield to the other, but I do know that members of the audience should not keep up a steady din or otherwise prevent others from listening to the speaker.

If all Harvard law professors talk and write like the dean, it's no wonder that faculty meetings have become a *cause celebre*, even in the pages of the *New Yorker*. Maybe frustration among the professors arises from their failure to communicate — even with one another — as well as from their political differences.

Things are not any better in the private sector. Here's a portion of the foreword to a law office manual, signed by the senior lawyer in the office: "Particular emphasis should be placed upon the description of individual and Section responsibilities. In that regard, early rapport with other professionals addressing similar legal matters may obviate duplication of effort and assure more expansive insight of a given problem under address."

Notice that all these passages share certain characteristics. They are impersonal, abstract . . . cold, almost incomprehensible. Sometimes representation of a client requires that kind of writing. But too often lawyers write out of habit, or because they don't know the difference. Why do so many people dislike lawyers? Lots of reasons, but many say that lawyers tend to be impersonal, cold . . . abstract, almost incomprehensible. So what's the answer? What remedy should Judge Weinstein have ordered?

Lawyers can be taught to write better. I present as evidence that it is possible the last quoted passage, which was surreptitiously slipped to me by lawyers who have been taught to distinguish between gobbledegook and clear legal writing.

WHAT IS PERSUASIVE WRITING?

Above all else, lawyers are paid to be convincing. Whenever judges or writing gurus lecture, they admonish lawyers to be persuasive. But what does that mean? Take a homely example from a commuter station: "To avoid payment of fare is a violation of law." This sign would hardly persuade a petty criminal to go straight. The verb "is" can't carry the burden of scaring off turnstile jumpers. Everyone exploits the verb "to be" unmercifully, using it to connect inchoate ideas floating around in our heads. It may be the perfect verb choice in "I think, therefore I am," or "God is love," or "The Lord said, 'Let there be light,' and there was light," but most of us are not so effectively philosophical.

The actions ("pay" and "violate") in the example are frozen into unpersuasive noun forms, or nominalizations. The warning is also purely abstract. Nobody and nothing tangible appears — not the potential crook, not the hoosegow. But it sure sounds lawyerlike. The lawyer or functionary who drafted that warning sign could have written a sentence with vibrant verbs and real agents: "If you don't pay the fare, you will go to jail." Perhaps the warning now oversimplifies the legal process, but it is far more likely to persuade.

One of my favorite examples of insipid, unpersuasive legal prose comes from an article on legal writing in *The Business Lawyer*: "One of the most persistent criticisms of the lawyer in action is that his writing is so poor, wordy, vague, uncertain." Had the distinguished lawyer who wrote that sentence not had his verbal rhythms destroyed by a lifetime of "reading law," he might have written it this way: "Lawyers are often criticized because they write in a poor, wordy, vague, uncertain style." Still not a masterpiece, but at least the sentence reads a little more clearly and persuasively. Note also that merely by putting the action in the verbs instead of in prepositional phrases, the sentence's word count is cut by one-third.

WHAT YOUR FIRM CAN DO

By now your eyes are no doubt glassy with boredom at reading bad prose. These examples were set out for two reasons: First, to demonstrate that the writing problem is real; second, to suggest that it is not entirely insoluble. But if you think the law schools are quickly going to solve the problem, forget it. Yes, the legal academy occasionally produces elegant stylists who are willing to teach writing like Harry Kalven of Chicago and Fred Rodell of Yale, but they are dead and who has replaced them?

Bright students enter law school with no worse literary skills than their peers. Many lawyers suspect, however, that students' writing skills decline during three years of reading judicial opinions, along with law review articles and other tortured prose offered up as the standard to which they should aspire.

The ABA has imposed an accreditation standard on law schools that obligates them to do something about writing, but the standard is vague and the blind have never been real good at leading the blind. An ABA committee chaired by Carl Felsenfeld, formerly Citicorp's vice-president for consumer banking, now a professor of law at Fordham Law School, is seeking ways to improving legal writing in law schools and could eventually make some headway — but law schools change very slowly.

That means lawyers are stuck with the job of solving the problem in their law firms. Yet nothing shakes a lawyer's ego more than the suggestion that he or she needs to repeat freshman English or seventh-grade grammar. After all, lawyers are paid to express themselves and most of their expression is in writing.

Nor is grammar their main problem. The examples above are not terribly ungrammatical. Lawyers regularly write sentences that are perfectly grammatical but also turgid, prolix, and unconvincing. These grammatical sentences are likely to be strung together in an erratic and disorganized structure that reflects the chronological course of the lawyer's research effort or his thought processes, rather than a logical and convincing flow of ideas and issues. Chances are that several firm partners would be delighted to lecture associates on good old-fashioned rules of grammar, but they all would waste valuable billing hours in the process.

The fundamental problems are stylistic and organizational. Unfortunately, these are much more difficult to correct. If the firm imports its local English professor, your colleagues might well savage him or her in their eagerness to argue about legal **175** terms of art and nuances of meaning. In such arguments, lawyers are extremely skillful at reducing nonlawyers to tears. In self-defense, the English professor will retreat into his or her arcane areas of expertise. Like ships that pass in the night, the lawyers will be arguing law, and the English prof will be spouting psycholinguistic jargon.

Define Goals

It's fairly easy to identify the basic qualities of good legal writing. Good writing helps clients, judges, and other lawyers understand the point of the text. It should be clear, direct, and precise. It must withstand attack from adversaries. Very often, it must be persuasive. Unlike the novelist, a lawyer usually intends to convey one meaning and one meaning only. In other words, much of legal writing is like reveille, not a symphony. It's designed to wake up the soldiers, not to entertain them. The goal is to minimize complexity and ambiguity — to keep it simple.

Brandeis said that there is no good writing, only good rewriting. Lawyers spend enormous amounts of time rewriting, whether editing their own work or that of others. Effective editing must also be a fundamental goal of a writing program.

These primary goals quite properly deal with quality. But don't forget productivity. Lawyers all have colleagues who turn out decent drafts — finally — but invest far more time than they should in the process. Lawyers waste considerable time as editors, too. Many senior lawyers themselves rewrite drafts received from associates. Although they know it's inefficient in the long run, they feel inadequate to the task of coaching their associates' writing. Think of the time lawyers spend writing and editing and imagine how a 2- to 5-percent productivity increase would improve a firm's bottom line. What if the firm gets lucky and obtains a 10-percent gain in productivity? It's not impossible.

Decide on Writing Program Participants

Firm management usually imagines that training programs are for entry-level lawyers. Don't automatically embrace this view, especially when the subject is writing. For several reasons, the firm may want to design a program for senior associates or — even better — partners.

Good writing programs use the actual work product of participants. Brand new lawyers have no work product. If they wrote law review notes as students, their own drafts were probably edited by platoons of other law review members, rendering those texts useless for teaching pur-

poses. New recruits also have their hands full learning the ropes of legal practice. They feel vulnerable enough without a writing workshop that will scrutinize their fundamental ability to express themselves. So they tend to resist and deny: reactions hardly conducive to successful learning.

Improving the writing style of junior lawyers may frustrate them if their bosses continue to insist on obtuse, ponderous, convoluted legalese. Writing is an art rather than a science, but it helps if people who disagree about style can argue about it in the same language. A good writing program provides valuable concepts and vocabulary for discussing style. If only junior lawyers understand the concepts and learn the vocabulary, they won't be able to communicate with their bosses.

A good writing program is largely about revision and editing. The more senior a lawyer becomes, the more he or she revises and edits rather than drafts. So the program is likely to be extremely valuable to senior lawyers.

A program for partners yields the biggest bang for the buck. If the program is good, it will improve supervisory lawyers' ability to coach the work of supervisees. This is a demonstration of the trickle-down theory that actually works. A program for partners also retains more value than one offered to young lawyers because more of the latter will leave the firm before it recoups its investment.

Determine the Extent of the Program

Some subjects can be taught effectively in one rousing lecture. Who can ever forget Irving Younger's sermon on the 10 commandments of cross-examination? It works on videotape and was awesome when he performed it for the National Institute for Trial Advocacy on a mountaintop in the Rockies. But writing skills aren't as easily acquired as the 10 commandments.

Learning to write and edit better and faster is more like learning a new tennis serve. A serve won't improve much through a Jimmy Connors lecture. A player will do better if Connors personally explains the new service, watches the player try it, and works with him on the court. And anyone is far more likely to develop a better serve after a series of weekly lessons from a merely competent professional instructor by playing as much as possible between lessons.

Mere lectures in legal writing may briefly stir the blood, but they are unlikely to have positive effects. One or two sessions that give participants a chance to edit their own works are better than lectures. But the recidivism rate will be unacceptably high. A writing program isn't worth much if it involves fewer than three sessions. Five sessions, each separated by a week, seem most effective, especially with a follow up session several months later.

Decide on the Curriculum

The market is flooded with miraculous techniques for instant weight loss, cellulite elimination, and sexual potency. So it's no surprise to find miracle cures advertised for flabby writing. They are called "readability formulas." Two of the most popular are the Flesch Reading Ease Scale and the Gunning Fog Index. Rudolph Flesch and Robert Gunning developed and popularized formulas that could easily and inexpensively gauge the difficulty of written prose. They insist that the difficulty of a text depends on two variables: sentence length and word length. Unfortunately, reading is too complex for any formula to predict readability with perfect accuracy. Mindless bureaucrats can use these formulas to prevent their prose from becoming absolutely impermeable. Lawyers, however, can't learn much about good writing from mechanistic rules.

A step up from magic formulas are the professors and journalists who have published variations on Fowler's *Modern English Usage* and Strunk & White's *Elements of Style*. A skillful writer certainly needs these two books in his or her library and would do well to add the legal gloss on them written by Professor Richard Wydick, *Plain English for Lawyers*. But neither these books nor public appearances by their authors go much beyond reminders to write clear, direct, forceful prose. Good advice, but no more helpful than Jimmy Connors's telling you to serve better.

Good writing and editing involve three elements:
- The overall structure and organization of a work
- The sequence and flow of ideas from sentence to sentence
- The internal structure of the sentence itself.

Lawyers have problems with all three elements, though some argue that the worst problem is organization. The bad news is that more is known about what makes a good sentence than about sentence order or the overall organization of documents. The good news is that the commonly known but often ignored outlines prescribed for legal memoranda and briefs conform to some of the best current linguistic thinking about discourse organization. Once they understand why Facts, Issues Presented, and Conclusions should precede Discussion, lawyers are more likely to organize their memoranda effectively.

An effective legal writing program deals with style and organization, but it also links the best current thinking about linguistic theory with the everyday problems of practicing law. For example, when should a lawyer stop researching and begin writing the legal memorandum or brief? At what stage of drafting a contract should a lawyer utilize forms? How can young lawyers convert from using pencil and yellow pad to dictating machine? Can lawyers harness word processors to help improve their legal writing and editing?

Even the best curriculum fails if not supported by good curriculum materials. Lawyers, like everyone else, practice denial. Because of their finely honed ability to argue distinctions where none exist, they may be better at denial than nonlawyers. So insist on curriculum materials largely derived from the work of lawyers taking the course. Otherwise, they will not believe the course is relevant to them.

Decide Who Should Teach

Find people who understand and can apply linguistic theory. If applied linguistic theory doesn't seem relevant to a practical course in legal writing, look at *New Essays in Technical and Scientific Communication: Research, Theory, Practice* (edited by Anderson, Brockmann, Miller; Baywood Publishing Company, Inc., Technical Communications Series 2, 1983), as well as Joseph Williams's fine little *Style: Ten Lessons in Clarity & Grace* (Scott, Foresman, 1981). But instructors also must know how a law firm operates. They should be tough and smart enough to take all that lawyers can give, but charming and witty enough to engage and keep their attention.

Even if a firm has lawyers who can teach writing and want to do it, consider whether it still should import instructors. Lawyers are, to a large extent, what they write. The introduction of a writing course inevitably provokes suspicion and hostility. Some lawyers perspire at the prospect of diagramming sentences (although they should not be asked to do anything of the sort). Former English majors and law review editors bristle at the notion that they have anything to learn about writing style. Many associates fear that they will be evaluated on their performance in the course. These problems may be compounded if the instructors are lawyers within the firm. Well-trained, competent instructors use a professional, nonconfrontational approach that ultimately diminishes the hostility of most participants. Lawyers become downright enthusiastic when they begin to see positive results.

There are excellent instructors, and they are very busy. Demand currently exceeds supply for instructors who fulfill the criteria laid out here. Teaching legal writing is labor intensive. It involves extensive preparation for each program, because the instructors must edit participants' writing samples and derive curriculum materials from them. Typically the format includes plenary sessions, smaller workshop sessions, and individual tutorials — an exhausting schedule for the instructors, less so for each of the participants.

If the challenge of establishing an in-house writing program is so formidable, continuing legal education organizations may seem to offer an alternative. A few have tried, including Massachusetts CLE and the Illinois Institute for CLE. Both efforts are serious and useful. (LawLetters cosponsored the Illinois CLE programs.) For lawyers in small firms, these programs may be the only game in town. But they are limited in several ways. They are usually too short. The faculty can't edit participants' actual writing samples. And these courses are likely to attract relatively large audiences, limiting opportunities for individualized attention. Theoretically, a CLE organization could offer a course that met all the criteria for success, but such a course probably would be no shorter or less expensive than an in-house program. To avoid publicly exposing confidential documents and the participants' own stylistic shortcomings, the course would have to be bland and pallid. So, if a firm can put together the resources, an in-house approach is likely to be best.

Muster Program Support

Support for poor writing programs or weak instructors cannot be sustained. The course must be damn good. Lawyers have a low tolerance for in-house programs that don't seem useful or are taught at the level of abstraction and leisurely pace of law school courses. Don't insist on homework or make-work in legal writing workshops. The course won't succeed unless it is based on the actual product of the lawyers' practice. But even without homework, a good writing course requires eight to 20 hours from each participant. Save your money if partners will irresponsibly pull associates out of the workshop sessions, or fail to show up themselves. This means convincing partners in advance that the course has value.

How? Autocratic edict works best but few firms are autocracies. Most are anarchies. So educate the partners about the value of the program. Don't just educate them about likely improvements in writing quality. Suggest how the firm's bottom line can improve if writing and editing can be accomplished a little faster as well as better. Before offering a full program, perhaps present an introductory session for skeptical partners. As long as they understand that such a demonstration only suggests what the entire course entails, it may help prevent wholesale kidnapping of writing workshop participants and disrespect for the course schedule.

It's not easy to square off against the legal writing problem, but don't be discouraged. It's not easy to diet or to provide high quality legal services either, but they can be done.

Decision Analysis: Pulling In Our Gut Instincts

Gut used to be good. It was OK if a little bit hung over our belts, and OK if we used it to estimate a client's chances in court.

Gut is not so good any more. Physically we run hard to get rid of it, and professionally our corporate clients demand more than our gut instincts about the outcome of litigation. Neither effort to get rid of the gut comes easy. But hard as it may be to forgo calorie-studded booze and desserts in favor of marathons and aerobic exercise classes, it's even harder to refine our gut instincts with systematic, quantifiable predictions about complex and uncertain legal disputes.

Still, belt tightening is the universal goal. Corporations are alarmed by growing legal fees, especially litigation costs: one general counsel said he gave his outside litigators an unlimited budget, and they exceeded it. So corporate policy makers increasingly see legal disputes as business risks involving not only the amount at issue but also legal fees, executive time commitments, public relations implications, the likelihood of success, and the present value of a possible victory years in the future. Whether and how much the corporation should spend on a dispute is becoming an investment decision not entirely unlike those made on product development or marketing, because the boss wants to weigh his investment against the probable return. Of course lawsuits bristle with unfathomable complexities and uncontrollable variables, but so do other business matters.

Nobody claims that legal disputes can now be run through a computer program that will produce evaluations as precise as your weight on the bathroom scale. But many business school-educated corporate managers are increasingly comfortable with analytic tools like decision analysis. And the principles and techniques of decision analysis have been transposed into the law. Used properly, they give us something more than gut instinct and vague assurances to cope with the complexities and uncertainties of litigation.

According to Marc B. Victor, a consultant and lecturer on the subject, "Decision analysis provides the logic — and the tools — for making good litigation decisions in the face of uncertainty." This system, Victor believes, not only will help our clients decide how much justice they want to buy and when they might profitably settle, but also will inform lawyers where to focus their pretrial discovery efforts, what trial strategy to employ, and whether or not to appeal.

"A typical decision analysis," writes business school professor Samuel E. Bodily, "forecasts the probability of each possible outcome and estimates its financial cost or benefits. Alternative strategies are evaluated in terms of their financial impacts on the company." Bodily reports that this system has been successfully applied in legal matters: one of the largest U.S. corporations may have saved hundreds of millions of dollars in damages and fees by settling for $50 million, a figure derived from routine decision analysis. ("When Should You Go to Court?", *Harvard Business Review*, May-June 1981, p. 104.)

The simple fact is that growing numbers of our business clients are uncomfortable without some quantitative forecast of litigation risks so they can make legal investment decisions roughly comparable to those they make in other high-stakes business matters. So we lawyers had better acquire the necessary tools to give our clients what they want. As yet, however, relatively few of us are comfortable with the tools of decision analysis — including me. Because there seems to be no way to explain decision analysis without describing it in action, I offer an oversimplified and hypothetical case to demonstrate its rudiments.

The Wherehouse Players, a Milwaukee repertory theater company, sued Lion International Films, Inc., producer of *Storm in Space*, for copyright infringement on the Wherehouse play *Space Wharf*. The suit was filed during production of the film, in which Lion was investing $25 million. Lion insisted that its screenplay was original and — in any event — was not at all like *Space Wharf*.

Lion was advised by counsel that a court would first determine whether Wherehouse's copyright was valid, and then consider whether the movie script infringed the Wherehouse play script. If infringement was found, the court would consider whether damages should be a fixed sum or a percentage of the net revenues of *Storm in Space*, a potential blockbuster. Industry custom and legal precedent suggested that an award would be no less than $50,000, or more than three percent of net. The lower figure represents the minimum that a studio ordinarily pays an unknown author for a "property." Three percent of net represents the maximum that a court is likely to award after finding willful copying of material central to a film's script. Lion's president, John de Snow, hoped the film would gross $80 million, but that was highly uncertain in the quixotic market of film. In addition to $25 million in production costs, he expected to spend another $25 million for a world-wide publicity campaign.

After giving his high-priced Los Angeles law firm some time to review the facts and the law, de Snow asked what Lion's chances were. "It's very likely you'll win," they said. As an experiment, de Snow then separately phoned each of the three litigators working on the case and asked what probability he would put on the "very likely" chance of victory. One said 85 percent, another 75 percent, and the third 60 percent. De Snow decided he needed more information, and — in the future — would be more careful in discussing cases with his lawyers.

The Wherehouse Players learned of *Storm in Space* coincidentally when a local movie critic, who had seen the play, was in Hollywood on a Lion International press junket. He noticed similarities and brought a copy of the movie script back to Milwaukee. The Wherehouse was a typically impoverished theater company. It had developed *Space Wharf* in workshops and had seen its play become the biggest hit in Wherehouse history; a Broadway production was not impossible.

When company members first read the movie script they were shocked to find scenes very familiar to them, *Storm in Space* characters that some of them felt were clearly inspired by *Space Wharf* characters, and passages of dialogue too similar to those in *Space Wharf* to be explained by coincidence. So Amy Sloane, producer of the Wherehouse, retained Jack Fastinato, an excellent intellectual property lawyer in Milwaukee. He was handling the case for 40 percent of any award. A good result for Wherehouse would give it needed financial stability, finance a New York tour, garner good publicity, and assuage the company's outrage at what they believed to be piracy.

Rather than risk losing a percent of the film's net to the Wherehouse Players, de Snow began to think about the cost of reshooting a few scenes to avoid any possible copyright claim. He also speculated on whether the case might be settled, and for how much. So when de Snow hadn't heard from his lawyers in a couple of weeks, he called another meeting to remind them that production was nearing completion, publicity was about to begin, and they had to act fast if changes were to be made in the film at a reasonable cost.

De Snow also said that he had personally read both scripts and was frankly chagrined at certain similarities. The lawyers shrugged and said if they offered any settlement now, no film would ever again be released without blackmail payments for alleged copyright infringements.

Furthermore, they had been in touch with the Milwaukee lawyer, Fastinato. He was a member of the Wherehouse board, devoted to advancing the arts in Milwaukee, and convinced that he would win the case. Lion International's lawyers believed that Fastinato saw this suit, if successful, as a potential annuity for his beloved theater as well as himself. He wasn't likely to be bought off cheap. Anyhow, discovery was just beginning and Lion's lawyers would know more when their experts had closely read and compared the two works and their investigators had ascertained whether the studio's writers had seen or read the Milwaukee group's play.

De Snow insisted, however, that Wherehouse and its aggressive lawyer might settle if they knew Lion would rather reshoot than risk having to pay them a significant percentage of the net. But his lawyers were reluctant at that early point to share Lion's entire game plan with the opposition.

Back in his office, de Snow, a Stanford business school graduate, decided to try a little decision analysis. To simplify the process, he set out to compare the approximate financial consequences of only two alternatives: offering a $100,000 settlement (an amount he viewed as somewhat less than the cost of reshooting the allegedly infringing scenes) or continuing to litigate. He drew a "decision tree" (Figure 1) to illustrate the financial effects of some options. The square box at the left is his decision point; the settle or litigate options branch from there. The litigate option has two liability uncertainties and two damage uncertainties. De Snow also lined out three outcomes for the film's possible gross, to help evaluate the cost of a percentage-of-net-royalty award.

The bottom line results of following each path are shown at the right end of each branch. The first column shows the fixed damage award payable this year. The second shows the variable portion, if the court awards a percentage of the net. The third approximates the present value of each percent-of-net award, discounted at 15 percent per year on the assumption that this part of an award would not be payable for five years. (A more sophisticated decision analysis might account for possible counterclaims, punitive damage awards, public relations, stock market implications of an adverse judicial decision, and management's value of its own time.)

Next, de Snow reflected that the probability of Wherehouse's winning would depend on the court's finding that 1) the copyright on *Space Wharf* is valid and enforceable, and 2) that

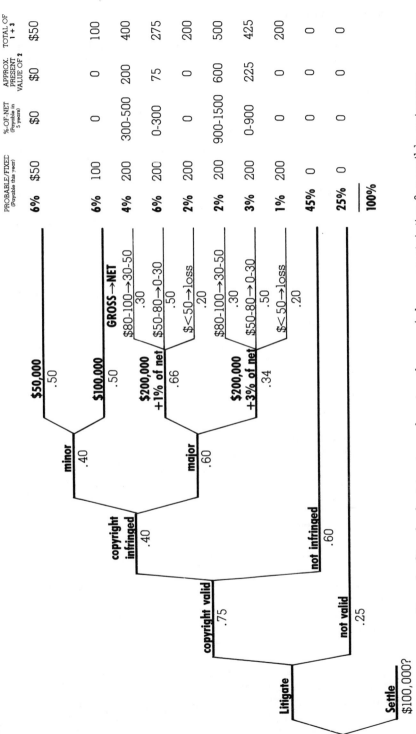

Figure 1. Simple decision tree showing the case's key uncertainties & possible outcomes

Storm in Space infringed on that copyright. At this point he went back downtown to his lawyers. When de Snow forced them to go beyond their initial "very likely" win estimates, they analyzed each element in the case separately. On the issue of copyright validity, they advised him that Wherehouse had produced *Space Wharf* without registering its copyright, but the script arguably carried a valid copyright notice. Lion would raise questions about the evolution and authorship of the *Space Wharf* script, which was created by many people pieced together over a period of time. So, they assigned a 25 percent probability to a finding that the copyright was invalid. On the issue of infringement, Lion's lawyers reflected on the chance of establishing that the similarities in the two scripts were no more than should be expected in the increasingly crowded science fiction genre. They believed the two scripts were clearly different in many respects (that the Lion script was far better written, for example). But several scenes did contain strikingly similar incidents. Moreover, three characters and several "interplanetary" words and phrases were virtually identical in the two scripts. On balance, the lawyers assigned a 60 percent probability to a finding of no infringement.

De Snow pointed out to his lawyers that the chance of Lion losing to Wherehouse was therefore only 30 percent — a 40 percent chance of infringement discounted by the 25 percent chance that the court would fail to find the copyright to be valid. Then, using LEXIS and the litigation department's experience with similar cases before the federal district judge assigned to this case, de Snow and his lawyers came up with estimates of what the judge might award Wherehouse upon a finding of infringement, depending on how significant the judge viewed the similarities in the scripts to be, and how willful he believed the infringement to be.

The movie studio's financial staff then showed the lawyers how easy it was to combine 1) the percentage probability of winning, 2) the probabilities of the various awards, and 3) the net present-value calculations. These were used to determine the probability distribution for the total cost of litigation at net present value. Figure 2 shows the likelihood that the outcome of the trial plus the anticipated $50,000 bill for legal fees would not exceed any particular value. This analysis yielded de Snow's reservation price of $100,000, the maximum that de Snow should pay to settle in view of the litigation risks and Lion International's attitude toward risk-taking. But de Snow's lawyers rightly pointed out that in negotiation, the reservation price is a *final*, not a first offer, so they invited Jack Fastinato to Hollywood for a settlement conference.

To de Snow's surprise and dismay, the case didn't settle even when negotiations led to Lion's offer of a sum very close to its

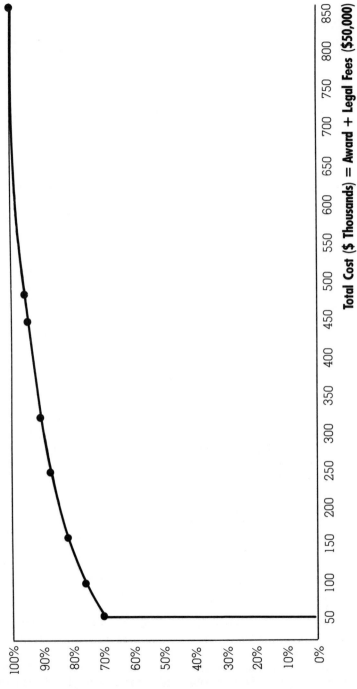

Figure 2. Probability of total cost not exceeding any given amount

reservation price. De Snow's lawyers said it was too early and urged him to relent and unleash aggressive litigation. But de - Snow suspected that the problem might be that Wherehouse's lawyer was working on a contingency basis. Because Fastinato had already spent considerable time on the case, his reservation price and Wherehouse's might be significantly different.

So de Snow asked his lawyers to set up another conference, this time inviting Wherehouse's producer, Amy Sloane, to accompany her lawyer, Fastinato. To distinguish this attempt from the failed one, de Snow and his lawyers suggested that a mediation service be invited to set agreeable ground rules and supply a mutually acceptable mediator. Fastinato was reluctant but he was assured the meeting was preliminary, the mediation was non-binding, and that it would all take place at Lion International's studios amidst the glitter of Hollywood. And it was winter in Milwaukee.

The mediator, retired judge Susan Albright, reviewed de - Snow's decision analysis and asked if she could share it with Sloan and Fastinato. At first de Snow's lawyers resisted, uncomfortable with the notion of sharing work product when they didn't have to. But she prevailed and patiently explained to the Milwaukee side of the table how the Lion International settlement offer had been determined by decision analysis. She reviewed Lion's analysis of the probabilities that the court would find an infringement. Then she added her own belief that the judge would be parsimonious in awarding damages.

Sloane and Fastinato were disappointed to learn that Lion could revise the script, reshoot some scenes, and avoid any possible infringement. But Fastinato urged Sloane to stand fast until he could proceed with more discovery intended to find an alleged letter to the Lion screenwriters that mentioned the Wherehouse play script.

The mediator explained to Fastinato that a probability analysis could determine the value of such information in this case. Finding such a letter might increase the probability of a Wherehouse victory from 30 percent to 60 percent, and thus raise the "value" of the case by $75,000. If the increased value of the case, discounted by the probability of finding the letter, were to exceed the estimated cost of the search, plaintiffs should proceed to look for it. (Such analysis may often determine whether specific discovery objectives are worth pursuing.) With Albright's help, this cost-benefit analysis was quickly done, and Fastinato himself realized how much *he* would be investing in a quest with so unlikely a result.

After a few more hours with mediator Albright, the parties settled near de Snow's reservation price — the final figure was $130,000. The additional $30,000 was added to Lion's reservation price after the mediator convinced de Snow that he should add value for several additional factors: First, Albright recomputed upwards the actual cost of reshooting to avoid the alleged infringements. Also, she suggested, reshooting the questionable scenes would delay the film's release approximately a year, and the fickle public — hungry for more science fiction films now — might not want *Storm in Space* when the remade film was finally released. Moreover, Lion's board of directors was currently adverse to this litigation because the studio had just been successfully sued by a star actor for padding expenses by millions before computing his percentage on the net of another film.

By the time of settlement, all the lawyers involved in *Wherehouse v. Lion* had come to appreciate decision analysis, although none believed it could resolve all disputes. Decision analysis cannot eradicate America's truculence and adversarial character, nor can it redistribute the unequal skills of different negotiators and litigators. But all agreed that it usefully harnesses gut instinct and supplements intuition. They were especially impressed by the avenues it opened to fruitful negotiation, in this case breaking an apparent deadlock after a first offer had been refused, simply because the parties could quantify the dispute's discrete elements.

This particular case might not have settled without a mediator, who was especially helpful because she understood the usefulness of decision analysis, encouraging both sides to fully exploit its techniques with her help. Basically, decision analysis gave the parties, their lawyers, and the mediator a framework for discussion that was unemotional, unthreatening, and nonadversarial.

According to Edward K. Hamilton, a Los Angeles consultant in dispute-related matters, "Successful use of any analytic aid to legal decision making must begin with recognition that the tool enhances human judgment rather than substitutes for it." But, Hamilton adds, "In the end, the lawyer's critical choices are still subjective." Decision analysis thus enables lawyers to measure objectively those elements of a case susceptible to measurement, and to compare their assessments in mathematical terms. "This does not eliminate subjectivity," says Hamilton, "it simply ensures that a lawyer's judgments (a) take into account quantifiable facts where they are relevant; (b) reflect a conscious effort to test the distinctions and gradations inherent in each predication by stating them in overly precise terms; and (c) hang together in a sequence that has tolerable systemic coherence and internal consistency."

A "perfect" decision analysis requires perfect judgment — now as ever impossible to achieve. Judgment will always vary among parties and their lawyers. Lawyers who want to fight will assign different values than those who want to settle. Parties with relatively great resources (insurance companies, for example) will be less concerned with risk than others, such as underfinanced individuals and smaller companies. And when one or another party believes that fundamental principles are at issue, trial and appeal may be inevitable no matter what the cost. An experienced mediator, however, is likely to minimize such aberrations by minimizing hostilities, examining parties' assumptions, and recalculating the probabilities realistically.

In the next few years, no doubt too much will be made of decision analysis. Some decisions — including but not limited to those involving morals, tastes, life, and death — simply cannot be quantified. But lawyers and clients together gain much simply by confronting that "30 percent chance" when it has been thoroughly analyzed and graphically portrayed. Similarly, when lawyers put litigation uncertainties and possible consequences on a decision tree, they are forced to address each issue and assess it in relation to the others. The way in which decision analysis structures and disciplines our thinking, rather than its numerical projections, may be its principal attraction.

Thus, however primitive and liable to distortion decision analysis may be, it is an improvement over intuition alone. And perhaps our reluctance to make systematic predictions for increasingly demanding clients has not arisen from any intellectually defensible rejection of decision analysis, but from ignorance and an inability to use its techniques. Now, however, we can employ them and offer the results for what they are worth, along with our insights, wisdom, and skill.